A
Wisp
in the
Wind

To Joel & Lisa —
  The answer is blowing
in the wind...
    look for it in Montana!

Many happy days

[signature]

A
Wisp
in the
Wind

In search of Bull Trout, Bamboo, and Beyond

Jerry Kustich

Illustrations by Al Hassall

West River Publishing

Published by
West River Publishing
P.O. Box 15
Grand Island, NY 14072

"Fifty-Fifty" and "P.S. Out Fishing" first appeared in _Fly Fisherman._
Portions of "Halcyon Dream" and "A Montana Mouse Tale" first appeared in _Montana Outdoors._
"The Diving Rod" first appeared in the _Power Fibers Online Magazine._

Printed in the United States of America

First Edition

10 9 8 7 6 5 4 3 2 1

Cataloging-in-Publication Data is available on file.

ISBN 0-9633109-4-1

For Dad, Ted, Ed, Bud, and all who have found that
working with one's hands is truly the gateway to the soul

Acknowledgements

When putting together a book, it is never done without a long list of supporters pushing it along behind the scenes. I would like to thank a few folks for their direct input. It was editor Kermit Hummel of *Countryman Press* who initially planted the idea for *A Wisp in the Wind* in my head. Dick Mitchell came along when we needed his keen editorial skills, but he has contributed many bits of wisdom to the work as well. Kathy Scott's eye for detail accompanied her many heartfelt words of encouragement. Al Hassall brought invaluable perspective to the project with his wonderful interpretive artwork. David Van Burgel served as a constant reminder of all those bamboo rod builders working in obscure corners of the country for the pure love of the craft. The "boo boys" and long-time friend Annette McLean provided much insight for the words I wrote from two decades of spirited conversation.

Others who deserve mention are the crew at Winston for keeping the hope alive by working more for pride than money; Tom Helgeson for his example of what a complete angler ought to be; Norm Zeigler for his constant reminder of how lucky I am to be living in Montana; and my wife Debra for her tolerance of the back of my head while I sit at the word processor in between so many fishing trips. Finally, a special thanks goes to my brother Rick for the decades that we have shared the fishing dream and his relentless effort to bring this entire work to a noteworthy completion.

Foreword

The bags were packed. This was it. This would be my first trip out West that did not mean sitting in the middle of a hotel lobby in downtown Los Angeles' business district. The itinerary: Buffalo to Las Vegas to Boise. Then, I would make the four-hour drive to Idaho Falls to participate in the 2003 Federation of Fly Fisher's Conclave and Ralph Moon's Bamboo Rod Symposium. Four hours? Was it worth the money that I saved by flying Southwest Airlines? It paid for the rental car, but I am still not sure.

As expected, the Symposium was full of wonderful bamboo rods and rod making, but it was Thursday's diversion to Montana that really left me awestruck. Robert Kope and I took off early in the morning to make a trip to R.L. Winston Company's wonderful bamboo rod shop, somewhere in the back streets of Twin Bridges, Montana.

I have known Jerry Kustich for only a little while now, but I feel like I have known him well for many years. We have passed once or twice on the lower Niagara River where big rainbow trout roam the fast running waters. Jerry has also been active in his brother Rick's *Oak Orchard Fly Shop* in Buffalo, a place where, I am embarrassed to say, I have spent way too much of my income on fly tackle. A few weeks earlier on the phone Jerry extended an invitation to visit the bamboo rod shop on this date. I was excited to hear that we would be welcome. He said not to expect to see master rodmaker, Glenn Brackett, but "you never know." Robert had also been corresponding with

Winston rodmaker, Jeff Walker, and with both invitations, we were confident that we would enjoy our stay.

When we arrived in town, there was no Jerry, but the owner of the local fly shop pointed us down the dusty street to the bamboo shop. He explained that we would probably see Jerry eventually, and then he reminded us that in Montana things run a bit more carefree than other places.

Upon getting to the shop we hesitantly peeked in to find that we had struck the mother lode. Standing there were Glenn, Jeff, and another man. They were talking and smiling, and we hoped that we had not interrupted a personal meeting. When Jeff greeted us and introduced us to Glenn and the stranger, Jack Howell, the author of *The Lovely Reed,* we knew that we had timed our visit just perfectly. After a few minutes of nervousness, Jeff began to show us around the shop, and the fun began. As it turned out, Glenn and Jack were just about to head over to Wayne Maca's shop down the street, so both Robert and I stayed behind to get the Winston shop tour.

Jeff Walker is truly one of the most gracious men that I have ever met. His sense of modesty and benevolence were impressive. It is no wonder that, as we later walked the streets with him, small children on bikes called out to him, "Hi, Jeff!" He seems like a legend in Twin Bridges, and after working for many years under Glenn, Jeff has gradually become a master rodmaker in his own right.

The thing about the Winston shop is that there is no "ancient Chinese secret." Every aspect of their shop and their construction seems open for discussion.

"Pictures?"

"Sure, go ahead."

"Secret varnish recipe?"

"Sure it's _____" (I am not telling you, go find out for yourselves)!

By the way, Jeff even gave me three pints to take back with me. They use one pint every time they spray, and use a new can every time. Heck, I am not so modest, I took three half filled pints! Thanks Jeff.

I stared at the milling machine for about ten minutes before Jeff explained every aspect of it. Robert and I also got to see some wonderful rods at all stages of completion that adorned the racks on Jeff and Glenn's benches (Note to self: make a rack for your bench, Bob!). The rods of several other makers were in the shop for one reason or another. We passed around a beautiful Michael Montagne rod between us, and saw several E.C. Powell rods in for repair.

Shortly afterwards, the three of us headed over to Wayne's little shop to catch up with Wayne, Glenn, and Jack. Wayne works at Winston but also operates his own business called *Beaverhead Rods*. I had only cast one of Wayne's rods prior to this. Jerry had brought one along to Grand Gathering in Fergus, Ontario in May. It was fast and light, and it was amazing! I looked forward to getting some insight from Wayne — a former snowboard maker turned rodmaker.

We watched as Wayne showed his blank making process, moving deftly between the belt sander, node press, band saw, and the *Tom Morgan Handmill*. He worked with an efficiency that only a professional builder attains. I really admired the ingenuity that he had displayed in the shop's layout and the making of the rods. We then cracked open a few beers and we chatted about rod making while the Winston bamboo production was grinding to a halt for the day!

After a while Glenn finally declared that he was off to, as he put it, "fish for his soul." These guys really do live life in a way much different from the fast paced life of the East Coast. I think Glenn meant exactly what he said that he intended to do, and I stood in awe for a moment wondering: "Where do I go to fish for that?"

We were fortunate enough to have Jack stick around, as the remaining five of us went out to cast some of Wayne's rods into the Beaverhead River beneath the watchful eye of the Twin Bridges water tower. Afterwards, we were off to Jeff's pizza parlor, where we enjoyed some of the best pizza I have ever had outside of Buffalo (we may have snow, but the food here is great). How do you beat a trip to Winston where you not only get to meet Jeff, Glenn, and Wayne, but you also meet Jack Howell — and, on top of it, Jeff buys the pizza and beer! Heaven really does exist on Earth, and it is the Winston bamboo rod shop in Twin Bridges.

Stuffed with pizza, we headed back over to the shop. I wondered why the drivers had stopped to let us cross the street. How did everyone in town know Jeff? Was that the beginning and end of town that I could see when I turned left to right? Where was the rest of it? How do I find a house out here?

Good old Jerry finally showed up and said that he had been checking on and off all day to see if Robert and I had arrived. Apparently we kept missing each other. We talked at great length about things back home, about the rod making business, and about Jerry's new book, *At the River's Edge*. (Robert and I, by the way, got our own signed copies before leaving.) Later, during the flight and connections home, I had the chance to read the book from cover to cover. In my opinion, it is one of the finest books about angling and living that I have ever read. It also started me reading one of Jerry's favorite authors, Roderick Haig Brown. *At the River's Edge* has become a very important book for me. Not only was it a fulfilling literary experience, but it was also a life-changing event. The book taught me that fishing is more than a sport, it is a pastime, a life worth living. I guess I had never realized the magnitude of fly fishing so clearly until I read Jerry's book.

We had arrived at just after 10:00 a.m., and now it was four o'clock. We had taken up nearly the whole day's work at the Winston rod shop. When in the presence of guys like these, their matter-of-fact ways speak volumes of their experience and commitment to rod making. They reinforced in me what I have believed for some time now; the best way to learn about rods is to simply keep making them. There is no tool, magazine, conversation, or book that will make up for time spent in the shop. For instance, Jeff's mastery has come from twenty plus years of doing a job — the job of making bamboo fly rods.

We headed towards the museum with Jerry, as Jeff waved goodbye and stoically got back to work. Robert and I eventually bid farewell to Jerry, and we took the time to visit the museum and look into the graphite shop from a window above the foyer. It had been a great day, one to remember for a lifetime.

The trip back to Idaho Falls was full of conversation about how wonderful the day had been going. It was filled reviewing tips and secrets that Robert and I had learned that day. We had a nice dinner and a few beers back in Idaho Falls, and all the while we shook our heads in disbelief over how gracious Jerry, Jeff, Glenn, and Wayne had been.

Bob Maulucci
Former Editor
Power Fibers

Introduction

My greatest fear in writing a book of this kind is trying not to sound like an old fart rambling on as if the only matters of importance somehow occurred years ago when I was younger. This is an ultimate concern to me, because what I write should speak as much to today's youth as it does to those of us who have admirably survived the gauntlet of many years. Understanding the role of tradition and history can tell us much about ourselves, but it is only in the context of our mortality that the continuum we call life makes everything we do come into focus. And one is never too young to grasp this reality. To the youth of today I say make the most of life by choosing wisely the paths that determine your future. I hope this book will encourage young folks to consider lifestyles that are unique, creative, and responsible. To elders I say don't put off until tomorrow those dreams you still want to pursue. I hope this book will prompt you to be a dream follower and, in the end, that you will share these dreams with the young.

Last year I read *Running Waters* by Bozeman author Datus Proper. Off and on, Datus would stop by the shop for a visit, but I always missed him. My goal for the summer was to give him a call and tell him how much I appreciated the book. In July, however, I was reading the outdoor column in *The Montana Standard* written by my friend Paul Vang about the passing of Datus Proper a few weeks earlier. To my regret, it seems that the author slipped on a rock while fishing a small stream, bumped his head, and succumbed on the spot. After another good friend died in

October, followed by my father's passing in December, my convictions about seizing the moment took on a whole new perspective.

I never knew Gary LaFontaine very well. And because of a lack of initiative on my part, I will always regret not finding more time to spend with Gary — not to mention hardly spending any time at all with other legendary fly fishing icons. It is only now that I realize what I have missed by not seeing the past through their eyes. And though Gary's contributions to the world of fin and feathers will never be forgotten, there is another aspect of his existence that should be highlighted. In addition to his tireless work that revolutionized the way we look at certain aspects of fly fishing, perhaps Gary's greatest legacy was the words of encouragement he shared with anyone who had a creative idea or dream.

In the early nineties my brother Rick self-published his first book, *Fly Fishing the Great Lakes Tributaries.* Shortly after its release, Rick was presenting the book to the public at the *Midwest Fly Fishing Expo* in Southfield, Michigan. It was there he met Gary LaFontaine. After careful scrutiny, Gary complimented Rick's efforts, and then he bought an autographed copy. "In order to be a successful author," Gary offered to my brother, "you need to publish another book within a few years. That will not only add legitimacy to this work, but this work will then call attention to the new publication." Because of Gary's reassuring words, Rick and I subsequently wrote *Fly Fishing for Great Lakes Steelhead: An Advanced Look at an Emerging Fishery.* It was released in 1999. Once again Gary was very supportive of this effort in the years of his declining health by positioning it, in his words, "on a prominent page" in his publishing company's catalog *The Book Mailer.*

I saw Gary for the last time in 2000 at the FFF conclave in Livingston. From his wheelchair Gary again urged me, as well as my brother, to keep writing. It was this final conversation with him that boosted my spirit to complete and release *At the River's Edge* in 2002. That book represented an attempt to integrate the lessons learned in a life of fly fishing with issues that should be important to any of us who try to find significance in the outdoor experience as it relates to water.

Gary never did get the chance to read *At the River's Edge*. But I am taking it on faith that he would have prompted me to write *A Wisp in the Wind* because there is still so much to share from a viewpoint that is truly unique. An angler's perspective from within the magical world of bamboo has much broader implications than what it would seem on the surface. And though fly fishing should be fun, it is also a serious pursuit in light of what is happening in the rivers that flow through our lives. This is not a book about bamboo rods. It is a collection of reflections and stories that give insight and inspiration to various aspects of life, including an undertone of encouragement of my own to everyone out there to do what needs to be done in life before it is too late.

Gary taught me that it is essential to motivate others, because, as in the Randy Travis song, "it's what you leave behind you when you go" that is important. Gary left behind many great works that include a great deal of insight about fly fishing, but most significant were the words not found in his books that urged me to keep writing what needs to be written. In this spirit I present *A Wisp in the Wind* — a book that should always be relevant as long as there are rivers upon which to cast our flies, and trout that are willing to rise to them.

Jerry Kustich
December 1, 2004

Part I

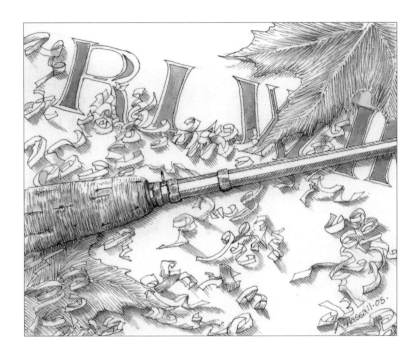

In a world where most days you have to settle for cheap merchandise made by robots and sold by surly zombies, some of us consider it an act of defiance to own something made by a dedicated craftsman who may well be working as much for love as money and who's proud enough of his work to sign it.

Fishing Bamboo
John Gierach

A Wisp in the Wind

I

Come on in! The door is always open — that is, when one of us is here. Sometimes we're all somewhere else, depending upon what's going on, but that's the beauty of working here. I'd like to give you an exact time when we will be around, but nothing is quite that simple at the bamboo shop. Be sure of one thing: If the door is unlocked, then one of us is here. Since it is a twenty-degree morning in December, there's a pretty fair chance that all four of us will be puttering around the shop at one point during the day. After all, the Big Hole River is clogged with ice jams and the lower section of the Beaverhead running through town is cold and tinged with brown; so it is not conducive to the even faintest of temptations. The Ruby and Madison Rivers offer limited possibilities for anyone looking to wet a fly during this late season, but the wise

21

angler would choose a day that rises above thirty degrees. Avoiding that annoying icy buildup after every few casts may be the least of one's worries once hypothermia starts to nip at the extremities. You can bet, though, there will be time for these considerations over the next few months, but today I need to work. There are strips to cut, and rods to build — and memories to ponder.

I don't usually get back to business until early December anyway. Whether traveling to the West Coast or taking a jaunt around the Great Lakes, most autumn seasons throughout the past twenty years have been devoted to my passion for steelhead. While other friends wander the mountains for elk or comb the prairies for birds with their canine buddies, it is the lure of the migratory rainbow that awakens a similar wanderlust in my soul. This is a journey I have grown to love, an epic sojourn that seems to be more about something other than catching steelhead. But this year, the usual fall routine was sadly altered when my father's health began to spiral downward in September, a vortex from which he would never return. Death and adjusting to it becomes a major part of living as one gets older. This reality hit home in early December when my Dad quietly passed away — one day after his eighty-fourth birthday. Two days after his burial I experienced one of the best days I have ever had for steelhead on the lower Niagara, the river that meant so much to our family as I grew up. It was a fitting way to say goodbye, since I would have never had this relationship with the mighty Niagara if my father hadn't built our home near its shoreline over fifty years ago. The next day it was back to Montana.

The best way to pay tribute to this fine man who loved to work with his hands, I figured, was to get back to work as soon as possible. Although my father didn't understand bamboo rods, he could relate to making them because one of his true joys was to work with wood. Whether it was remodeling the house or building a quaint knick-knack shelf, he was at peace in this domain. So here I am, less than two weeks after his death, working with my hands in a way my Dad would be proud of, on an instrument that elicits so much awe and mystery in the world of fly fishing. And since he knew how much fly fishing meant to me, I believe he would truly appreciate the significance of my gesture.

It is curious how much I rely upon walking next to a stream to seek comfort, consolation, and meaning. I once thought it was pure escapism, but now I am not so sure. For me, taking along a bamboo rod not only heightens the significance of the experience, but somehow the soul of the universe seems a bit closer with a wisp of cane in my hand. In the realm of Zen, the highly sought after state of contemplative illumination occurs only when one is free of exterior thought, influences, or any of the constraints associated with religious beliefs. *Where are you between thoughts?* was a question once presented to the luminary thinker Joseph Campbell by a wise sage on a pilgrimage to India. In Zen, Campbell concludes, it is only in this "between thought" state where *nirvana*, or true understanding, can be achieved. In the seventies cult classic *Zen and the Art of Motorcycle Maintenance* author Robert Pirsig delves deeply into the philosophical anguish that once drove him to the brink of insanity, using the motorcycle as both a metaphysical and pragmatic tool in his search for enlightenment. Following his arduous thought process to understand a confusing intellectual past, I came to the realization that the harder you try to get somewhere the more you get nowhere. In many ways I have been very fortunate. When I ask myself *where am I between thoughts?,* it is either building a rod or fly fishing

— a state of being where time stands still and everything makes perfect sense.

For these reasons I suspect that the bamboo fly rod has become a unique locus for those who have stumbled upon this same reality with regard to fly fishing. If this pursuit is an escape that can truly illuminate the humdrumness of existence and elevate it to a level of significance, then so be it. Although this analysis may be a bit overdone in the minds of some, unquestionably the activity we call fly fishing provokes more literature and subsequent discussion about the ethereal than any other recreational pastime known to mankind. Indeed, there are those who believe bamboo rods, fly fishing, water, nature, life and death are intrinsically linked, and that the very consideration of this connection may well be worth the effort. A bamboo rod may not be the only mantra, nor fly fishing the only path, as Pirsig's motorcycle quest would indicate. But if any of these concepts makes a tinge of sense and you find yourself wondering *why bamboo?* then stick around and spend some time with us. We love visitors.

Our shop is less a workplace than it is another world. Upon crossing the threshold, you enter a dimension more akin to a fairytale — a sort of "we're not in Kansas anymore, Toto" atmosphere that is as lost in time as the actual craft of bamboo is time-honored. It is like visiting the *real* Santa's workshop where one would expect to see little hobbit-like elves scurrying about the floor or standing at a bench pounding on this or sanding off that, but instead you will find only us. With graying beards, exploding hair, and a collective appearance that could pass for the reincarnation of *Lynyrd Skynyrd*, about the only situation Glenn, Jeff, Wayne, and I would comfortably fit these days is a seventies reunion rock concert or within this forgotten back alley building in Montana.

Upon first impression, it is apparent that the shop is more than just a collection of lathes and other outmoded machines, relics from an era when computers were merely the figments of a *Clockwork Orange* imagination. This is an eclectic Mulligan stew of sentimental artifacts and memorabilia collected over decades and arranged haphazardly in between stacks of papers and magazines, catalogs, order forms, sawdust, varnishes, tools, old rods, new rods, broken rods, and so on. There is a place for everything, and everything is in its place, a simple system of organized chaos. The main room is painted a dingy yellow, and along with the few flickering florescent lights humming a monotonous din in the background, one gets the feeling that this would be a perfect setting for a black and white *film noir* from the fifties; the only image missing is Humphrey Bogart puffing a cigarette in the dark shadows. The walls are covered with "a this" here and "a that" there, and the plywood floor is filled with equipment and other oddities separated only by narrow walkways to get around. To the casual observer this is a magical mess that represents more than a workshop. We can see it in the faces of those who drop by. It has been called a museum, a library, a sanctuary. But mostly, a holy place.

At certain times of day or night we are convinced that there are spirits dwelling within the old building. The walls resonate with the activity of thirty years. The floors creak with memories, the ceilings sigh with forgotten dreams. Natural light pirouettes off the dust-speckled interior like tiny ballerinas, a sepia-colored stage where the complexities of a confused society melt in the presence of integrity and cower in the face of truth. The four of us have become unified in both commitment and ideology over the years. We believe in goodwill. We believe in freedom of expression. We believe that God gave humans a brain to avoid the lockstep tyranny of manipulative leadership — political or religious. We believe in the Einstein quote that "peace can never be achieved through violence. It can only be attained through understanding." And we firmly believe that it shouldn't take an Einstein to know what the quote means. We sing to Dave Mason, the Doobies, or Zeppelin and Clapton, and hum to Vivaldi or Earl Klugh. At times, tapes of Dalai Lama, Joseph Campbell, or Deepak Chopra play in the background. In this win-or-lose, black-and-white, bring-it-on kind of society where kindness and understanding is considered a weakness, we stand for lofty ideals because that is the only way the world will change. A guy once died on a cross because he believed in the same principles. We often discuss the hypocrisies of the mean-spirited, self-righteous element in this country who say one thing, do another, and would likely crucify the same prophet they pray to on Sundays if he ever dared show his face once again. We are not religious, but we could not do what we do without a spiritual commitment to all that matters. A bamboo rod is an intense labor of love, and, like a sponge, it can absorb all these intangible layers of energy only to be released one day in some of the most beautiful places still left on this planet. And, by the way, we are totally committed to preserving these beautiful places, too, so that others may one day plug into this vast source of energy.

There are a few things you should know before you start to watch us work. In the 1881 *Book of the Black Bass* author James A. Henshall M.D., considers the bamboo rod "the greatest invention ever made pertaining to the art of angling, equaling the invention of the breech-loading rifle and shot-gun for field sports." Although the idea of split bamboo originated in England, it was perfected in America and became an American institution by the end of the nineteenth century. It is important to understand the bamboo rod in this context because one of the charms of building them in the twenty-first century is to preserve this American tradition in a modern day art form.

Even back in 1881 Dr. Henshall credited Samuel Phillippi of Easton, Pennsylvania, as the originator of the American split bamboo rod. That distinction has held to this day. Charles Murphy of Newark, New Jersey, followed with creations of his own until Hiram Leonard from Bangor, Maine, came onto the scene about 1870. Considered by some as the "Father of Bamboo Rods," it was Leonard's six-sided configuration and subsequent techniques for production that revolutionized fly fishing by making rods available to the sportsmen of that day. Until the advent of fiberglass rods in the sixties and graphite in the seventies, split cane rods were the industry standard if you wanted to fish. Throughout the twentieth century many production companies popped up that were able to mass-produce practical and affordable "fishing poles" of all kinds. During that period, as well, fly rods of higher standards were also built by individuals or small groups, many of whom were disciples of Leonard. Other builders popped up here and there, too, and names like Payne, Edwards, Garrison, Dickerson, Gillum, Powell, Young, et al. became synonymous with quality cane rods in the nineteen hundreds. In the collectible market, rods built by any one of these masters are now worth a great deal of money.

With the onset of synthetic materials, however, the demand for bamboo rods declined tremendously and only a relatively few individuals and a handful of companies persevered to make them in the latter part of the century. The 1969 upstart Thomas and Thomas, Powell Rod Company, Orvis, and the Winston Rod Company were among the small number of major players that still continued a remnant production rod for the die-hard follower. Hand-crafted rods were also available from seasoned artisans building them in obscure shops tucked away throughout the country. Since this is not intended to be a detailed history lesson, I should mention here that there are several good reference books available for those interested in the entire history of the bamboo rod — including all the companies and notable builders. Suffice it to say that the bamboo rod has stood the test of time and is still a wonderful tool to elevate any experience at the river's edge. But these days it has also been transformed into a symbolic expression that connects the origins of American fly fishing to the present in a way that far exceeds any practical value.

During the early nineteen-nineties there was a notable resurgence of interest in the bamboo rod. Whether it was an increased number of retirees who grew up using cane or just a growing number of anglers frustrated by the limited capabilities of the lighter and faster characteristics of graphite, basement rod builders and hobbyists started to pop up all around the United States and Canada. Armed with hand planes and V-grooved adjustable steel blocks, many started to reproduce rod tapers handed down through time by the twentieth century masters of the craft. Information gleaned from a growing number of books and knowledge shared by journeyman builders at annual conclaves and gatherings provided the impetus for these budding craftsmen to head to their basements or garages and start building. Shops were improved to accommodate the many phases of building or new ones were constructed from scratch. The resulting work has been admirable on many levels. I have met some wonderful folks within this circle of bamboo artisans in recent years. They have kept the spirit of bamboo alive, and those of us at Winston appreciate the renewed interest they have stimulated in the bamboo trade.

Many of these builders elect to limit construction to just a few rods per year for themselves, or to share with friends and family. However, this resurrection of cane enthusiasm has also spawned a new-age cottage industry for those willing to work hard in exchange for somewhat dubious financial returns. There are now rods available on the Internet in all price ranges. But since not all rods are created equal, a good rule of thumb for buying a new rod these days is that the price tag should reflect the longevity, recognition, and reputation of the craftsman. Presumably, a guy who stands up to the test of time only does so because of the quality of his work and the dedication to the craft. This assumes, too, that he will be around in the future if something does go wrong. When you figure that one individual working full-time may be able to produce only thirty rods or so per year, do the math when considering the price — especially, when the costs of building (including excise taxes) are figured into the finished product. People will often ask, "Is a bamboo rod worth the price?" The Zen response would be *you have already answered the question by asking it.*

Back at the shop you can see me standing there at the milling machine with my back toward you. Other than my height advantage, Glenn and I could pass for brothers. Because I am writing this, it is my prerogative to say that our grayish beards and full heads of longish hair make us look distinguished in a professorial kind of way. Glenn is the oldest and wisest of the crew, and has been building bamboo rods now for over thirty years. He is across from me, stooped over, making the final adjustments on the dial before the machine starts to *whirr* and the vacuum begins to *rev* into a loud whoosh. If you were actually at the shop, we wouldn't be able to talk for a while, but you could surely watch if you wanted.

It doesn't seem possible that so many years have passed since I walked into the shop to meet Glenn in 1984. I had just moved to the area a few months earlier to fish as much as possible, but the need to eat was also a serious consideration. Originally, my intention was to find a guiding position, but after Glenn sized me up, he recommended against that idea. He had gone down the guiding road himself, and concluded long beforehand that it is a tough one. "I can tell, you like fishing too much," Glenn stated from a voice of experience, "and guiding can taint your passion because it is an all-consuming job." After talking at length, Glenn then suggested I come to work at Winston. It would only be part-time in the beginning, but then, he said, I could fish as much as I wanted and make enough to get by. But since my wife would be doing some teaching as well, at least we had our foot in Montana's door. Over twenty years later and I am still holding Glenn to his word — that is, about fishing as much as I want. If Glenn ever regrets the offer, he never lets on.

Today we are cleaning up some odds and ends. The first batch of strips that Glenn is preparing has already been rough cut with the milling machine to a triangular shape and subsequently baked so each strip has been tempered and given the desired color tone for the finished rod. Backtracking a bit, the original strips were directly split from a culm of Tonkin cane grown in the Canton region of China. Bamboo is actually a member of the grass family that grows to maturity in five years. There are hundreds of species of bamboo growing around the world, but Tonkin cane has emerged as the best for the construction of bamboo rods, replacing Calcutta cane from India used in the nineteenth century.

Rod builders work with the woody rind on the circumference of a hollow stalk that is two to four inches in diameter. This is dense material with fibrous veins that run the entire length of the culm. Although bamboo is a particularly strong and elastic substance employed for many purposes, it is normally utilized in a natural state, or roughly split. The wispy strips rod builders whittle from the outside edge is perhaps the most elaborate use of the material, carving it down to the essence of what makes bamboo so enduring. These power fibers are the soul of the bamboo rod.

Those who work with wood believe the material possesses an inner life that bridges the craftsman to the natural world in a unique relationship. Although bamboo is different from true wood in some respects, working with it is very similar. Whether the artisan carves a fish, or builds furniture, a musical instrument, or a bamboo rod, the end product can be as inspiring to those who obtain the crafted object as it is to those who create it. For those who appreciate the finer qualities of wood, they can perceive a heartbeat in a finished work of art. The musician can feel the instrument breathe, morphing eventually into an extension of one's being. The bamboo aficionado senses true harmony with the universe as a fly is cast into the sweet song of a beautiful river.

One by one Glenn will feed a five-foot triangular length through the mill and I will pull it out along with a cam or template that will tilt the anvil upon which the strip is sitting into the cutters. This puts the first taper into the strip. The machine is started. A test strip is pushed through. It is measured and the machine adjusted. Another is pushed through and checked. Then another. Glenn stops the process and fiddles with cleaning the cam and the area around the feed. Any dust buildup — even a speck — can throw off the exacting measurements that we seek. Another passes through. Glenn fiddles some more. I check my finger for a cut. The edges of the strips are as sharp as a razor, and the splinters easily sink into the fleshy parts of the hand. Finally, we get on a roll. My mind starts to wander seeking that state between thoughts, but with an unsettled world, four years of drought here in Montana, and the death of my father gnawing at me, there is just too much to think about.

In 1974 Glenn helped Tom Morgan move the Winston Rod Company from San Francisco to this very building in Twin Bridges. In 1991 they sold to a fourth generation of ownership. A new facility was built in 1995 on the outskirts of town where the finest quality graphite rods are now built. In 2004 the company celebrated its 75th anniversary and our shop continues to move forward today as one of the longest continuously running bamboo operations in the history of the fly fishing industry. We are still considered a production shop, although not in the traditional sense when rods were cranked out of factories in large numbers. In a way, we are kind of a hybrid where certain duties are shared by collective hands, but they are all done under the close scrutiny and watchful eye of Glenn's expertise right on down to the very finished product. Other well-known rod makers like Leonard, Payne, and Young have employed this same strategy in the past. Likewise, throughout the history of Winston very few other hands touched the rods during the reign of the original owner, Lew Stoner, and his successor, Doug Merrick. When former Winston employee Gary Howells went into business on his own in the early seventies, he once wrote about his rods to *Fly Fisherman* that "I do all the work myself, and I machine my own reel seats and ferrules. No other hand touches one of my rods before it leaves my workshop." This statement best summarizes the main difference between the true individual rod maker and the team effort of a production style company where somewhere in the process all of our hands have touched the work.

Glenn is still feeding the strips and I am still pulling them. We are a few hours into the cutting. So far we have passed the small pile of sticks through at two different settings. There will be one more pass before they are set aside. These are destined to be #11 tips. The number "11" corresponds to the finished ferrule size that the six strips will represent when glued together. In this case the resulting blank will require a male ferrule with an 11/64" diameter. Out of the corner of my eye I notice Jeff working on something at one of the lathes. He is tall and burly, with bushy curly hair and a lumberjack beard. He would be intimidating if he wasn't such a gentle giant. Jeff has been at Winston for twenty years too. Although I moved into the bamboo operation in 1992, Jeff has been here his entire career. He is a whiz with machinery, and his love for building anything is evident right on down to the exactitude he brings to a finished rod. In between working at the local pizza parlor he built with his wife, they are now working on a self-sufficient solar house in the nearby sagebrush-covered hills, and his mountain-man appearance fits the part perfectly. Jeff's pursuit of this dream reminds me of the six years I once spent in an isolated cabin in Northern Idaho with no power or running water. Sometimes I wish I could go back.... My mind wanders thinking about it. For years, that was home — and home is wherever the mind can return for comfort.

I guess I would have to say that the best aspect of our involvement with Winston is that it does not require a full commitment of time, but it does demand total dedication of heart and soul. With the exception of Glenn, who never seems to leave the shop, Jeff has the flexibility to build his home. I can write, travel, and fish, while Wayne, whom you haven't met yet, can work on his own rod company — and fish. We adjust our pace according to the workload, and do our own thing in between. This is a good arrangement for each of us, but even a better one for the company. In the winter, however, we try to get ahead and do some work that will make our jobs easier when the few months of good weather arrive in the summer. One of them is cutting and gluing strips. We are nearing the end of our third pass. One more strip and it is done. Glenn shuts down both the mill and the vacuum. The shop is silent until Jeff greets us back to the land of the hearing. As Glenn begins to change the cutters for the batch of butt sections, the back door jingles to announce a visitor.

II

It is half past noon and we figure it must be one of the locals stopping by for lunch break. But when the footsteps finally attach to a face after the few seconds of lag time it takes to walk through the entry room, we are all pleased to see Wayne step into the shop. He looks particularly chipper today with trimmed hair, sculpted beard, and a new fishing hat all accented by a pair of glasses, a Cheshire smile, and hair that shows no gray anywhere. That's not saying much since he is a bit younger than the rest of us. He is wearing a sweatshirt with the *Cruise or Bruise* logo that was the name of the snow board shop he owned in Idaho Springs, Colorado, and since the outdoor temperature has risen to a balmy twenty-six degrees, his feet were still bare tucked within his sandals. Lately Wayne has cloistered himself within the walls of his shop a few blocks away; so we haven't seen him much. He is hopeful that this monastic devotion will soon result in a few finished rods that can be promptly distributed to the waiting public. Wayne has been working with Winston for over six years, but his main goal since moving here from Colorado has been to set up his own small rod business. Although his intentions have been clear right from the moment he moved into town, Glenn figured it wouldn't hurt to capitalize on Wayne's talent in one way or the other — that is, if he was willing to share it.

Wayne is a character with an interesting past. An accomplished fine artist and composite engineer by training, he was among the first wave of pioneer snowboarders to hit the slopes of the western ski resorts in the early eighties. Subsequently, he used his knowledgeable ability to both design and build some of the very first commercial snowboards ever to swoosh down the mountainsides of Colorado. After burnout set in from dealing with the "corporate greed mongers" and "pompous profiteers" that eventually inundated that industry, he decided to give it all up in the mid-nineties in favor of applying the same snowboard technology to bamboo fly rods. His desire to design a durable, light, and moderately fast action rod incorporating the esoteric qualities of cane with space age wizardry never available to the innovators of the past caught Glenn's attention. As an established master of the craft, he is astute enough to understand the value of someone's trying to go where no one else has ever gone before. In fact, Glenn's unconditional encouragement may be the greatest gift he has given any one of us. It costs nothing to encourage a person to follow one's dreams, he figures, but the consequences could be profound.

"How's it going, Wayne?" We all chirp in unison.

He just shrugs, taking a sack from under his arm and placing it upright upon the cluttered file cabinet. In almost the same motion he pulls out two cans of beer, one in each hand, from the pockets of his fleece vest. Putting them down, he pulls out two more. Jeff then slips the contents of the brown paper bag out into his hands and asks, "What's the occasion?" It is a bottle of *Jack Daniels*.

"My fiftieth birthday today," Wayne tips one of the cans that he just popped open toward us.

"Here, Here!" I say, grabbing one of the others while toasting the hallmark. I add, "You don't look a day over forty-nine!" The fact is, he looks much younger than that, but there's no sense flattering him too much.

"Yea," Wayne chuckles, "not bad for a guy whose friends thought he would never make it past thirty-five." He was referring to a reckless past and his compulsion for living on the extreme edge.

"What the heck," Jeff chimes while opening the JD. "According to Jimmy Buffet, it's always five o'clock somewhere! Here's to ya, Wayne!" He takes a swig. The rest of us just gulp beer.

"Since the government already thinks I'm dead," Wayne pauses, "every year that goes by, I figure, is a bonus anyway."

Wayne was referring to an official notice he received from the Department of Social Security when he was eighteen declaring something to the effect that according to their records he had officially died at one point during the year. Understandably, he was upset to hear about his premature passing, and much time over many years was spent trying to undo his greatly exaggerated demise. "If you think the government is difficult to deal with when you are alive," Wayne quips, "try doing it when you're dead!"

And though he acknowledges that there are advantages to being a statistical nobody, Wayne also realizes the dire consequences inherent within this predicament when he reaches retirement age. That's why he'd like to set himself up to build rods until he's ninety. After we make another toast to his miraculous resurrection, Glenn fits the housing back onto the milling machine. It was time to get back to the task at hand.

This time around we would be cutting butt sections for five strip rods. For many years I have had an affinity for "five-strippers", but don't ask me why. All I know is that the very concept of this unique configuration has always been very appealing to me. Since it has never been my custom to take the road most traveled anyway, building a pentagonal rod, if nothing else, would be a fitting exclamation point to my out-of-the-mainstream approach to life. So in 1995 Glenn and I experimented with the idea. At that time we decided to make a prototype for donation to the local Trout Unlimited fundraiser, and it turned out to be a very pleasant feeling rod. Since then I have continued to dabble with the notion.

A few winters back Wayne invited me to use the *Tom Morgan Handmill* at his shop for further experimentation. I bought five-sided cutting blades and took Wayne up on his offer. Tom Morgan is Glenn's former partner as owners of Winston Rods. During his years at the company, Tom became a well-known rod designer, and the unique action he developed in the original Winston graphite rods still has relevance in today's market. After selling the company in 1991, he subsequently used the same ingenuity to design a revolutionary new-age milling machine to cut bamboo strips that is moderately affordable to the average person, and fairly easy to use. The Morgan handmill is a cross between a hand plane and a motor driven milling machine — blending the concept of both into a device that is efficient and exacting. This machine still requires the sweat of one's brow to operate, but it is not as labor intensive as a hand plane. I spent a month of evenings milling one strip after another until I had enough to build several prototypes.

A Wisp in the Wind

During that time Wayne and I discussed the practicalities associated with a five-strip rod. Since all four of us at the rod shop are in constant dialog about rods, or fish, or other important matters, this kind of discussion was commonplace. In fact, Wayne's mind thrives on dissecting the innards of just about anything — functional or figurative — into many pieces in order to gain a clear understanding how it works. Although Wayne wanted to see me build a pentagonal rod, and he was completely supportive of my effort, I could tell he had his doubts about the project. As an engineer, he pointed out that five-strip construction really doesn't make much sense. If one takes the cross section of a blank, he pointed out, it is easy to see that it is not symmetrical. One flat doesn't oppose another flat as in the six and four-sided configuration; instead, the flat with guides attached is opposed only by a glue seam in the pent design. In Wayne's hypothesis, that means the mass of the blank on the side with the guides is not counter-supported by an equal and opposite mass and, thus, will eventually break down. Wayne wasn't alone in his theory. This was essentially the same argument Everett Garrison made when he denounced five-strip rods years ago.

Garrison was not only a highly regarded hand-plane artisan from the thirties, but he was also an engineer. His word was respected and, consequently, may have discouraged other builders from giving five-strippers a try throughout much of the century. Claude Krieder and Nat Uslan were two who did buck the trend, however, and both built rods that were highly regarded. These days there are several individuals around the United States and Canada who have found five-strip rods appealing, just like I do, and they all believe that the glue seam (with today's glues) opposing the corresponding flat may have a bridging effect that more than compensates for the mass issues.

Anyway, it makes for good debate, and the butts we are cutting today will put us one step closer in a plan to offer an official five-strip Winston Rod sometime in the future.

It is easy for the mind to slip into contemplation at the milling machine with ear-plugs dulling the sound of the equipment and repetitiveness lulling one into a hypnotic daze. I feel like I should be sadder about my father's death. But instead I now seem very much in tune with his spirit as my hand grabs another strip and pulls it toward me together with my other hand guiding the cam. Maybe George Bernard Shaw had it right when he wrote: "The best way to seek God is in a garden. You can dig for him there." Although my father liked to catch fish to eat, he didn't find much sense in recreational fishing. So I know he didn't recognize a spiritual value in angling. What he really loved, though, was to work in the garden when he wasn't building something with his hands. Thus, maybe, without even knowing, he was in touch with the Eternal. Then again, maybe he did know it. In this same respect, it would be difficult for me to believe that I am not presently in touch with my father in the same creative realm he loved.

Back at the Winston shop, I look across the machine to see Glenn pushing through another strip of bamboo. Building bamboo rods is something I do, but for Glenn, the "bamboo way" is something that has become synonymous with his existence. After thirty years of devotion to a craft he obviously cherishes, here is a man who has been transformed into a being who emanates an aura of positive energy that spills over to anyone who stands near him. It may be difficult to believe that building bamboo rods could possibly have anything to do with the kind of person Glenn has become, but one only has to consider Glenn's credo that working with the hands frees the soul. The forces that truly can make a difference in this world, he believes, are locked deep within every individual. The trick is finding the key. For him, it is bamboo. And every time one thinks about it, here we are, back to Zen. There is something about bamboo rods — making them and fishing with them. There is something about fly fishing. What it is only becomes clear in the activity itself.

In *Zen and the Art of Motorcycle Maintenance* Robert Pirsig found poetry in his motorcycle. He endeavored to feel the ebb and flow of its parts as if it were a living being. He was one with it and knew it down to the last bolt. Conversely, his creative traveling partner could not care less about his bike and would only confront it when the machine was broken. Pirsig seemed to have a great deal of trouble understanding his friend's romantic way of looking at things and concluded that there must be two distinct approaches to life. The technologist deals with life from the perspective of nuts and bolts, and the artist deals with it from a standpoint of feeling and expression. One is concerned with form and function, the other with mind and being. Pirsig tormented over finding the commonality between the realm of technology and science and the realm of romance and art, and this seemed to be the main thrust in his quest for meaning. His obsessive compulsion to make sense out of life's every last detail could have driven anyone to the edge. Somewhere in between that old Nike slogan "Just do it" and Pirsig's need to understand everything right on down to the tiniest atom lies "the answer," that is, if this kind of answer is important to anyone.

Pirsig would have loved the world of bamboo. Historically speaking, most masters of the craft were accomplished technicians and machinists concerned mainly with the production of a utilitarian commodity to sell so that they could feed their families. Although they put a lot of effort into making a quality product that was as perfect in appearance as it was in function, ultimately, to them it was *just* a fishing rod. Many anglers back then were folks like my father who weren't as openly concerned with the significance of a fishing life, though, intuitively maybe they were. But sometime after the onset of graphite rod production, the perspective changed. Nowadays the modern craftsman devotes much time and effort to creating a work of art that preserves all the romantic dimensions of the bamboo rod. This is not to diminish a builder's technical talents, or to imply that these very rods do not function superbly. But it does point to the evolutionary shift of thought from the consideration of a bamboo rod as a practical tool to a bamboo rod as a tool of essence. This delicate blending of technical with art is the ground of commonality where two very different worlds have come together.

One only needs to look at our shop for further insights. Glenn is about beauty and grace, and though he capably deals with technical issues, what he ultimately creates is a work of art that truly comes from deep within his being. Then there is Wayne whose mind is always chewing on some technical issue — a better way to do this or a revolutionary approach for that. In the end, what he produces is a wonderful expression of his technical genius and magical talents. Jeff is a mechanical mastermind who is able to translate the "ebb and flow" of machinery into a creative masterpiece that reflects his in-depth understanding of both metal and wood. As for me, I am on a need to know basis when it comes to technology. At best I am a bamboo dabbler who loves to fly fish. My talent lies in writing about the spiritual connection between both. Collectively, our parts add up to a synergy that is undoubtedly reflected in the rods that come out of our shop.

As we begin to make the third pass on the five-strip butt sections after Glenn's last dial adjustment for the day, I become entranced with the quaint charm of our comfortable workplace. Details become more apparent as my mind tries to shed its present burden. Next to the place where we are standing, the milling machine rests upon a cement pad positioned at an angle so that the puller can operate free of the clutter that occupies much of the area. The machine itself is one designed by original Winston owner Lew Stoner. Although it was totally rebuilt by the mid seventies, the remnants of Stoner's original mill are now in the museum at the main Winston facility. The cement pad is big enough for two lathes as well. The rest of the floor is just plywood that has worn through a lamination or two in several spots from the many years of foot traffic. Excess glue left over from our assembly sessions is systematically poured here and there to patch the areas that show the most wear and tear. The main shop is small and compartmentalized. There is also a back room that contains the *South Bend* lathe, the oven, and Wayne's work area. Additionally, there is a separate coating room, a spray booth, and an entryway with storage capacity for blanks and strips. Twelve-foot culms of cane are kept in a warehouse across the street.

To my right is a bench that stretches the entire length of the shop's west side. Glenn's workbench occupies the northern-most portion of that space. There, thirty or so rods stand on a rack against the wall in an order known only to Glenn. Some are in the final state of completion. Others are set up for repair or refinishing. At one time or another there always seems to be an old Leonard or Payne needing a little work. The space overlooks a courtyard with a few trees planted for departed friends. There is no view other than the neighboring storage facility made of corrugated steel. Though totally uninspiring, on special afternoons that corner of the shop transforms into a magnificent shrine of devotion. This happens when rays of soothing sunlight drift through the window like strings of cosmic energy, embracing Glenn in an aura of soft yellow light that accent the browns and tans on his bench in a surreal snapshot of a man immersed in true bliss. The scene could just as easily be from the nineteenth century.

To my left, as I pull another strip through the mill, stands the *Enco* lathe we use for ferruling the blanks, and beyond that is a *Craftsman* lathe used for sundry purposes. Then there is a narrow path that borders another long bench upon which lies the ancient wrapping machine. This clever device along with the small drill press made from a sewing machine motor are the only two pieces of equipment left that Stoner himself used. Because of the connection, Glenn loves to work with this antique piece of equipment to wrap guides on the blanks. Over the years I have wrapped thousands of rods using a very simple tension devise in the comfort of my home. I never did learn to operate this old machine, which, when used properly, can wind three-strand dainty free-standing wraps perfectly over the ridges of cane.

Beyond that bench is the long coffin-like nook Jeff claims as his work area. There is a portal from that room opening to the main shop. Although it is tight quarters for a big guy, I am sure the view of the snow covered Tobacco Root mountain range more than compensates for the confinement. Right now you can observe Jeff trying to tweak the tip section of a ferruled blank to make it a tad straighter. My bench on the southeast corner of the room is sandwiched between the bookshelves that we like to call our library and a showcase that is our shrine to

A Wisp in the Wind

Gary Howells. Gary was Glenn's close friend, and, as stated earlier, he left Winston in 1970 to become a renowned craftsman of cane toward the end of the twentieth century. Although Gary did his work in the Bay Area, he spent many summers in Twin Bridges. Our memorial contains his picture, fishing vest, flies, and a couple rods. My window looks into the yard of the county's highway department shop where there is usually a huge road grader blocking any view.

On the walls throughout the main shop is a gallery of photos, drawings, art, letters, and poems. Friends, family, and fish adorn the photos. Drawings from Glenn's kids are posted in many places, and there is also a large picture of Roderick Haig-Brown and a framed shot of Sid Eliason with a beautiful Ponoi salmon. Specially tied flies are randomly scattered about, too. One shadow box contains a fly tied — without a vise — by the distinguished West Coast steelheader Harry Lemire. Also, high upon the wall hangs crusty old Bertha, the thirty-inch brown trout Glenn caught in a much younger day on California's Hat Creek in the sixties. You could spend hours looking, reading, and wondering what it all means. Some folks do.

The cutting session is coming to a close for today. At one point in the buzz of noise and the intensity of concentration Wayne finished his conversation with Jeff and then slipped back to his shop. Shortly afterwards Jeff took off for a very late lunch. The final pass of each tip section will be done tomorrow. The five-sided butts will need one more cut before they are ready to hollow. The pieces have become smaller and more fragile in appearance. It is hard to believe that this high-speed hunk of metal can reduce a giant blade of grass to such a delicately tapered strip of exactness. What once stood as a wisp in the wind growing tall on a hillside in China is now destined to one day return to nature as a man-made tribute to all that is beautiful.

III

You could take every peaceful town ever depicted on every Christmas card ever produced and none would compare to the serenity of Twin Bridges in winter. Located just above the confluence of the Big Hole and Beaverhead Rivers, Lewis and Clark passed right through here over two hundred years ago. The town stands like an oasis amidst a vast expanse of pastures and meadows. Modest little houses and a bunch of hand-planted trees adorn the few gravel roads that connect to the paved two-lane which doubles as Main Street for about a mile. In every direction you will see mountains, although the Tobacco Roots to the east is the only range close enough to actually reach out and hold the town in its embrace. The velvet layer of white as far as the eye can see this December provides a psychological respite for ranchers and sportsmen alike after four years of serious drought, but no one would be foolish enough to believe that our worries are over yet. Setting aside these concerns, the aesthetics of such scenery at this time of year is like listening to a perfect song when you need to hear it.

The town itself doesn't look too full of life anymore. After the state closed the local orphanage in the seventies, businesses shut down and not much has happened ever since. But if you scrape the surface a bit you will find a varied gathering of townsfolk who would rival the lovable characters found in that mythical TV town of Mayberry. In fact, in the summertime you kind of expect to see Andy and Opie whistling their way to the shore of the Beaverhead in a flashback that would seem more fitting to our way of life than the actual realities of a modern society creeping closer with every passing year. We have artists and craftsmen, fishing bums and guides, writers and dreamers, ranchers and cowboys, and a lot of very nice women named Betty. Despite many differences of opinion among the residents, every one gets along very well because we all have learned to sit down and discuss varying points of view. To my knowledge not a disparaging word is ever spoken about anyone else. Well, sometimes my wife may have something to say about me, but only when I deserve it.

There is nothing quite like taking a winter walk to the outskirts of town at midnight when the stars shine so crisply that the snow reflects the glitter of a trillion light years like infinite specks of magic dust. It takes just a five-minute stroll to be totally engulfed in a vast silence broken only by the yip of a coyote or the hoot of a great horned owl. Getting to the base of the mountains would take another twenty-five minutes, but for now a walk to the foothills will do. For thirty years I have lived on the edge of a vibrant emptiness either here in Montana or in the wild regions of Idaho, and I have often wondered why such openness makes some men so uncomfortable. In fact, these visionless folks can't seem to rest until the wondrous void is filled with massive monuments to mankind's machinations. Rather than face the emptiness with the courage it takes to hear what the earth is trying to say, they try to fill every open space with buildings and noisy machines so that all opportunities for anyone to plug into the wisdom and power of the universe are ultimately stifled. In this era, it is so important not to lose the few special places we still have left. When I look up past the stars and feel within myself the force imparted by this awesome power, the sensation is overwhelming.

After all these years I am no longer afraid of the night either, and if a mountain lion or a wolf would ever take me off to dinner during one of these walks I couldn't think of a more fitting way to return to the earth. Upon looking back toward the lights of town at midnight there is not a vehicle to be seen or heard anywhere. To capture the feeling and express it would be like trying to show someone a moonbeam in a jar. After every long trip outside of Montana to fish or, in this case, deal with my father, I have to find a way to check reality upon my return to be sure that being here is not just fantasy. But for every journey I make as I get older, the more memory, reality, and dreams merge into a singular consciousness. A walk like the one tonight puts it all into perspective. Life, death, and everything! It is so quiet and still that I could fall to my knees at the altar of this natural cathedral under the sheer magnificence of its spectacular splendor.

The 2003 Winston catalog features a panoramic black and white view of Main Street, Twin Bridges taken on a morning this past summer when the slanting shadows cast by a budding sun drape the sparse collection of buildings with a gentle aura of peacefulness. There is not a car in sight except for a 1952 Plymouth sitting in the foreground. The photo is a timeless depiction of small town Montana that could just as easily have been taken fifty years ago. I am reminded of the sixties *Twilight Zone* episode "A Stop At Willoughby." After a rat-race of a job took the main character to a near mental break down every day, he awoke one evening from a nap on his train ride home at a station in a mysterious little town. The twist: Willoughby was a stop back in time at a turn of the century place where being good neighbors and the concept of community still actually meant something. After several days of the same occurrence, as the story went, the character eventually yielded to temptation and finally got off at that town in the past, never again to return to his meaningless modern-day existence. I look at that shot of Twin Bridges and realize that I regularly climb in and out of that photograph as if it were my own personal "twilight zone" where imagination, fiction, time, and real life are but a blur.

If you stare at the picture long enough it might take you back in time to see Joe Brooks getting ready for a day on the Big Hole or Charles Kuralt stopping by to pick up his mail. There is Scott Waldie, the former owner of Four Rivers Fly Fishing Company, talking to his wife Jane who operates the Old Hotel Restaurant. Scott has written two wonderful books about the make-believe Montana town he calls Travers Corners, but it bears a remarkable similarity to "Twin," as it is called by locals. My wife is heading to the library. Norm is putting out a sign in front of his Weaver's Studio. Marge is running the flag up the pole at the post office and Mac is strolling back to his grocery store. There is one of the Bettys taking a walk with her husband. You can almost smell the coffee brewing and bacon sizzling in the Blue Anchor as the aroma wafts through the morning stillness. If you continue to look hard enough you can see Glenn carrying a bundle of split cane from the warehouse behind the library to our shop across the street. Here comes Jeff on his bicycle with a packaged rod under his arm on the way to be shipped at the main Winston facility. It is a picture of a thousand words — and many stories.

I am reminded of the July day in 1993 when I took my two nephews who were visiting from California to the section of the Beaverhead behind the library. It was their first experience fly fishing and by the end of the afternoon we were able to figure out a few techniques that allowed each of them to land his first brown trout ever using a pale morning dun. I am also taken back to a hot August

48

morning three years ago when the clouds of tricos were so thick that it was impossible to distinguish any imitation on the water. It was my pleasure to fish with Joan Wulff and Annette McLean that day. Like me, Annette has been at Winston for twenty years, and she is now the production manager. After observing her function around the factory, I have determined that Annette has to be one of the more clever women in existence. We get out fishing together every now and then, but despite great plans, it has been far too few times throughout the course of two decades. That morning all three of us were casting our flies along the stretch of Beaverhead that flowed through the shadow of Twin's water tower, but the fish weren't impressed with Joan's prowess, Annette's cleverness or my feeble attempts to explain such persnickety behavior. In such fine company, though, being ignored by all those whitefish and a handful of fussy browns just reaffirmed the fun of the challenge and the importance of good friendship.

I look into that photograph and can see the hordes of Mothers' Day caddis swarming around town on a warm April afternoon. There's me running across the road toting one of Glenn's quad creations in eager anticipation of a predictable certitude. The fish in the town stretch would be rising, because they always do during this event, and for some reason this piece of the lower Beaverhead always seems to have more fish in it at this time of year than there should be. The day that this early caddis hatch doesn't awaken my inner child and make me act like a school kid once again is the day the story will be over.

And it is all about stories — fly fishing, bamboo rods, and life itself. Maybe this is why the panorama of town moves me so, because contained within are generations of stories that can take one to another side of existence where life is always good and truth is not wrapped in a web of contingencies and compromises. Within that world life can be anything you chose. A recent TV drama *DreamKeepers,* written by John Fusco, tells of an elderly Native American impassioned with keeping the folklore of his vibrant heritage alive so that the future generations of *all* peoples can benefit from the insights contained within his stories. At one point Old Pete Chasing Horse queried his grandson about what would happen to all these tales after he passes to the other side. Chasing Horse asks, "Who will tell the stories, who will keep the dream?" And I wonder. As fly anglers we learn techniques, we tie flies, we discover new places to go, but in the end it is the dream we are chasing, the story that will take us somewhere else that isn't here. In the end the story is all we have, and if we don't pass it on, there will be no dreams left either.

Glenn and I get out on the water together less and less these days. I remember one time in the early nineties after I had been zapped by a bad batch of epoxies at work when Glenn took me to Fan Creek in Yellowstone National Park. His act of friendship was my salvation, and the warning of prowling grizzlies combined with finding some westslope cutthroat in the meandering meadow stream sure beat all the remedies known to modern medicine prescribed up to that point. It was one of those memorable days when the hatches continued to bring fish up all afternoon, and, as an added bonus, we didn't get attacked by a rampaging bear. For this reason Glenn likes to round up the 'boo boys" at least once a year for a pilgrimage to a local river. It is just good medicine.

A few Octobers ago we all headed up to a friend's property on the upper Ruby River with a few beers in the cooler and the prospects of sharing a fine day together in an early fall setting. To our pleasure, the aspens were still decked out in an array of shimmering yellow and the junipers stood proud upon the hillsides like chubby monks dressed in dark green robes. The earthy smells that whisked from the surrounding hills were dominated by the sweet fragrance of Douglas fir. The day was warm, but the chill emanating from the shadows was a good indicator of the cold nighttime temperatures that regularly occur at this time of the year. Before dispersing out of the driveway in varied directions we each discussed our choice of flies for the day. Glenn was going to fish the riffles with a small riffle-hitched black streamer that he had concocted. I decided to look for some subtle sippers using a diminutive green-bodied Adams. Jeff opted for the standard Royal Wulff and Wayne whipped out his highly touted creation: The Serial Killer. This marabou-covered, rubber-legged, foam-bodied monster could scare a moose, but it has also caught a lot of big fish. *Denver Post* outdoor editor Charlie Meyers made the fly famous in one of his pieces that summer and Wayne had been filling orders ever since. Wayne grumbled incessantly about the time it was taking, especially when there was good fishing to be had. "That's what you get," I said, "when you create a world famous fly. Everybody wants one! Oh, and by the way, do you have any extras?"

Jeff walked upstream with his six-stripper. Glenn had his quad. I had a five-sided prototype, and we both walked to various sections downstream. Glenn was accompanied by his American Eskimo dog, Sitka, a rolly-polly eruption of white fir with an attitude. Wayne would take his super-rod to the section of river in front of the cabin. The water had a distinct chill. In fact, it was damn cold. But some *pseudocloeon* duns were slowly riding the gently moving slicks, and a few of the uneducated rainbows rose to take my imitation. At one point I was able to watch Glenn from a distance and noticed his rod bending here and there. After several hours had passed I came upon Wayne fishing an upstream bend. To my amazement, he had been wading the forty-degree water all that time in shorts. For a guy whose winter footwear consists of putting socks on under his sandals, this shouldn't have been too much of a surprise. When I approached, his legs were splotchy pink and varying shades of purple, but the wetness on his shorts judiciously stopped below his crotch. His face wasn't blue yet either.

"How's the fishing?" I asked.

"Not bad. The Killer moved a couple nice ones."

"Cold?"

"Not bad." The words rolled out of his mouth like slow pouring molasses.

"How's the new rod working?"

"Not bad." Wayne was modestly living up to his extreme reputation. Just looking at him, I was shivering by association. Of course, this is nothing compared to some of his harrowing springtime fishing jaunts down the Big Hole in a canoe. Come to think of it, you can add me to the list of those surprised he made it past thirty-five.

After the sun's descent behind the mountain cast a cool blanket across the entire valley, we all arrived next to Glenn's suburban at the same time. Jeff had such a good day with his Royal Wulff that he figured this outing should last him for at least a few years. He was serious too. When it comes to fishing, a little goes along way with Jeff. The rest of us were quite satisfied, and Wayne immediately grabbed a beer to warm up. Glenn's familial obligations had limited his time on the water the past few years, so I know he probably treasured this day more than any one of us. It doesn't ever take much for the "boo boys" to make a toast, and this trip inspired a simple one.

"To a great day on the water," was Glenn's heartfelt proclamation. Sitka acknowledged with a royal "wuff" of his own, and we all clunked our beer cans together amidst some idle banter about the color of Wayne's legs.

Reflections like these are the riffles in a river flowing from the past to the present as a continuum of stories that are forever with us. These considerations subsequently become the foundation for all that is important in later life — memories, dreams, and transcendence beyond the mundane.

At a recent Solstice celebration with a few friends, our host started to regale the gathering with a few insights about growing older. This retired philosophy professor from the University of Montana has also written nine books about the origins of philosophy and other related matters. As well, I might add, Dick is a devoted fly angler who shares the same passion for Rock Creek near Missoula as I do. When he quietly started to speak, we all turned our attention to the scholarly man.

He talked about the dynamic aspects of growing older, particularly in his own life, and the consequent need he was feeling to face his approaching mortality realistically. "In youth we spend more time doing and less time thinking," he conveyed. "In later years we spend more time thinking about all that we have done and less time doing more." With a bit of sadness he regretted that the fallout of age progression in his life has been spending fewer days on the river. The upside, he continued, is that his sense of revisiting the past through the process of remembering was now more acute than ever, and he postulated that maybe this ability evolves in the human as one gets older. We all discussed that concept and concluded that perhaps this reflective stage of development results in wisdom, and the urge to share it. At one point in his discourse Dick implied lightheartedly that a good idea for the last book in his series of works would be a philosophical treatise from the banks of Rock Creek. Although the rest of us expressed the hope that this wouldn't be his *last* book, his point was philosophical, as one might expect from a guy with Dick's background. "It is important," he concluded with conviction, "that we all leave behind a completed story of our lives so that others may learn from it."

Relating this to my life, I knew exactly what Dick was talking about because it seems that I live now more in the past than ever. As he indicated in his discourse, certain smells, sights, songs or sounds can trigger a wonderful trip to rivers in the mind without ever leaving home. Although I fear losing the desire or ability to actually be somewhere doing something, the past, present, and future have now become so fluid that everything seems like a story.

Maybe this is why I have become so fascinated with fishing stories over the past few decades. I like reading them. I like writing them too. Ancient cultures once told stories that could be easily remembered and conveyed by word of mouth. These myths, parables and fables were created and evolved for the purpose of connecting generation to generation over time in a bond of spiritual oneness. The truth within these stories was the message, and eventually many were written down for the benefit of modern mankind as well. In today's society, however, multi-sensory technological advances have overloaded our capabilities with so much information that we now seem to be out of sync with this aspect of the past. Simply stated, we have lost touch with our story. Immediate information at the press of a button reigns, and anything that has to do with a universal truth stretching across generations would appear to be adrift in this vast sea of excessive data. At least to me, the fishing story is still a remnant throwback to a time when simple words kept folks in contact with basic truth. Although fishing stories are intended to inspire one to go fishing, they more importantly encourage an appreciation for the total experience of life itself. In what I write, "live the story" is the most essential insight I could ever pass on to the next generation. For as Old Pete Chasing Horse stated in *DreamKeepers:* "A people without stories is like wind blowing in buffalo grass."

IV

This morning we will be making the final cuts on the number "11" tips. Hope you can make it again. Additionally, we have to hollow the butts to make for a lighter, quicker section when the five-strips are finally put together.

Upon entering the shop, Sitka derives great delight from blocking my passage into the main room. With a barrage of barks and a pose of intimidation, the cantankerous canine stands his ground. I have learned to grab a milk bone out of a conveniently located box and bribe my way into the inner sanctum, a tactic that seems to work. Sitka has also learned the benefits of panhandling. I am convinced that was his plan right from the start. Though the old boy has mellowed at this mature stage in life, I'd hate to be there the day we run out of milk bones.

Actually, watching the cutting process for any length of time would be rather boring because of its redundant nature. The best time for a visit is when we are working at individual tasks throughout the shop or gathered to glue up the strips and bind them together to create a finished blank. This will happen either tomorrow or the next day. At that time anyone is welcome to hang around, to either join in on the conversation or ask whatever questions come to mind. A person could even choose a CD to play in the background, if one so desires. Most folks are surprised with how much information about rod building we are willing to share. There seems to be an impression that this is normally a clandestine sort of affair where work is done only at certain phases of the moon in a candlelit room filled with burning incense. Although it is not uncommon for Glenn to light a sprig of sweet grass from time to time and let its ghostly essence swirl like a specter of good luck throughout the building, he also insists that there are no secrets in our shop when it comes to building rods. "All the tips or magical insights in the world can't replace devotion, dedication, commitment, and gumption," he will say, "and there is no secret in that."

We would also like to dispel any myths that bamboo rods are built by grumpy old men in shadowy places for a snooty class of anglers. Whereas this characterization may ring true in some instances, many builders, including those of us at Winston, would like to reach out and encourage more folks to experience the joys of bamboo — certainly not drive them away. Despite the regrettable cost barrier that is prohibitive for many folks, this doesn't mean we can't share our knowledge and enthusiasm for this tradition. For those interested, though, there are also some options for finding an affordable way into the bamboo world. In Glenn's mind it is not only our mission to help out in any manner possible, it is our legacy.

Glenn has wrapped yesterday's strips in a damp towel so that this final cut today will pass smoothly through the milling machine with no frayed edges. The dampness eliminates much chipping and splintering. This final pass has to be perfect or a finished blank may reveal a visible glue seam that would render the section useless by our standards. The #11 tips are the first strips on the agenda. The initial one is passed through the high-speed cutter, and it is pulled slow and steady to avoid any breakage. Glenn checks the measurement of the whisker thin piece, an adjustment is made to the dial, and then one more strip passes through. When Glenn is satisfied with the exactness of the measurement, the routine begins.

One by one by one, frail-looking pieces tapered thinner than toothpicks emerge from the machine as I put them in a loose pile to my right. Although this may seem like it would be a boring task, one of the most enjoyable elements of working with bamboo is that we never look at the clock. Time moves along like a meditation in a steady but meaningful way. This is in sharp contrast to some of the jobs I have had in the past or even days spent in a classroom when it seemed that the clock was stuck in mud. Although the concept of time has fascinated thinkers from Aristotle to Einstein and beyond, on the surface it doesn't seem that there would be much to think about. There are only twenty-four hours a day and seven days a week to work with during our lifetime. In one respect it is a fixed amount, an unavoidable constant that could seem suffocating to the human spirit if dwelled upon too long. The one wildcard in this equation of constants, though, is that the human race has devised ways to gain more time by figuring out better ways to live longer.

The only problem now is that we try to jam so much into life by choice and by necessity that it flies by faster than ever before. Multi-tasking has become the buzz of the twenty-first century. A fast food burger in one hand, a cell phone in the other, and a race to another important appointment — all in the same motion — defines modern existence. The irony here is that a longer life in this age may even seem shorter than a shorter life span in the past. Thus, time becomes an interesting concept.

In the book *Sacred Time* author Gary Eberle explores the notion of horizontal time and vertical time. Horizontal time is the clicking of the clock as we speed through a day doing a zillion things or, or in some cases, slog through a day trapped in a tedium of boredom. Moments come and go in succession until the day is over, and then, the next morning the process starts all over again. Vertical time, though, are those periods in life when the clock seems suspended in a timeless experience where hours fly by almost unnoticed. This occurs when one gets lost in something that is truly enjoyable and worth doing. In vertical time the experience is eternal in nature, and fulfilling in every way imaginable. It is not that the clock doesn't tick on by during this state, but the perception in terms of the horizontal is that it was time well spent. Eberle postulates that this is the realm of sacred time, a timeout from time, a realm that can make life spent clicking off horizontal time much more bearable, and immensely more consequential.

Simply stated, it is not as much a matter of slowing down the hands of time as it is using the time we have more significantly. One of the goals, of course, would be to allow for more periods of sacred time in one's life. For me, bamboo rod building is an opportunity to kill two birds with one stone, so to speak. I get a chance to work as well as spend sacred time all in one effort. In this medium time is a steady flow of what it should be, and it is very comfortable and even more significant. I neither feel cheated about time lost nor regretful that I should have been doing something else. But when it comes to fly fishing, I have to admit, there does seem to be a problem.

We are nearing the end of the 11's. Since Glenn has another dozen or so to push through, I probably have another few minutes to explain my concerns. In terms of vertical time, for me a day spent along a river becomes a soulful state where the mind and body seem transported to an eternal universe that is the source of great peace and enlightenment. But before you think I have gone off the deep end, consider that many others have experienced the same phenomenon. For example, author Dave Aimes in *A Good Life Wasted* observes: "Fishing well requires an utter concentration that somehow slows the hands on the cosmic clock. Einstein showed that time is relative to the fabric of space. Depending on factors like acceleration, time slows down and speeds up like a car, and when time stops there is only the moment." And though this ethereal experience can occur in other outdoor or creative endeavors, fly fishing's uniqueness lies in the fact that it can lure an individual into a desire for habitual periods of vertical time on a regular basis. Thus, we get to the enigma I just mentioned.

Days fly by faster than the speed of light in terms of horizontal time when one is fly fishing. In fact, there seems to be no accounting for the passage of hours on the clock. In theory, if a continuum of these days were strung together, life would be over in a blink. Maybe this is the basis for that old saying that God doesn't deduct the days we spend fishing from the total time spent on earth. The concept would seem to imply that the only way to counteract the effects of time vaporization with regard to fishing would then be to find a way to extend the life of a fly angler by another hundred years or so. But then, the only way this time expansion would work is if the angler would agree to refrain from casting a fly on about half of the years allotted. The conclusion I come to, as Glenn turns off the mill and vacuum, is that the issue of time isn't as elementary as one would think. In fact, you can now see why thinkers throughout the ages from Plato to Jung could really sink their teeth into the concept. A modern theory believes that the mystery of time perception is a function affected by neurological changes brought on by meditation, chants, religious ritual, or any other inducements that naturally alter the state of consciousness. Add fly fishing to the list, although the Buddhist monk lost in some sort of physical contortion that elevates him to a plane of soulful awareness may suggest that it isn't quite that simple.

" They look good," I say to Glenn.

" It went very well," he replies, "these should glue up nicely."

Glenn removes the housing covering the cutting blades. These will be replaced with the cutters designed to grove out the apex of the butt section, thereby creating a hollow in the assembled blank. While Glenn deals with this matter I go to my bench and prepare ten five-sided butt sections that had been finished on the *Morgan Handmill* and now need to be hollowed as well. These are carefully marked so they don't get mixed up with the others that we ran through yesterday. While standing at my bench I greeted Jeff and asked him about the condition of the road up to his house, since it has been snowing a bit for the past few days. One of the drawbacks of rural living can be unplowed roads. Although Jeff indicated that the seven-mile gravel thoroughfare to his property was still quite passable, his life style reminded me of the times that I regularly had to walk the last mile to my northern Idaho cabin in the mid seventies when heavy snow began to fall. Mine was not a county road, so it never got plowed.

I told Jeff about the day "way back when" I hiked out to my vehicle one February to go fishing for whitefish and the possible westslope cutthroat in nearby Priest River. This was an activity I would do several times a week until my Forest Service job would get going again later in the spring. The hike was through a thick forest of lodgepole, firs, and birch. In the boggy areas there were spruce and cedars. The truck would be parked in an open pasture hidden off the main road, and it often had to be dug out from the snow that would regularly fall. Going fishing in the winter was always a monumental effort back then, and after a day at the river it was just as easy to procrastinate in the local bar rather than do what it took to get back to the cabin for the night. One evening I had one too many beers with my hippie friends and shot one too many games of pool with the local logging contingent so that getting to the cabin was even more of a challenge than normal. Since I never used a flashlight, I couldn't tell that the plank-bridge crossing the deep hole on the brook trout stream bordering my property was covered with glaze ice. Slipping into the water upon the very first step was truly sobering. After carefully crawling out of the waist deep hole and making my way through the snow and freezing temperatures to the cabin, where there was no fire, I had to resort to all the Jeremiah Johnson skills I could conjure. It took a while to get the wood stove going under those circumstances, and another several hours before the stone cold cabin would warm enough to thaw my bones. Although I wouldn't trade those days for all the money in the world, I told Jeff that living in town nowadays was just fine with me.

I then brought up the dilemma I was having about time and fly fishing. We often carry on long discussions about all kinds of issues that range from Montana's weakened water standards to the dumbing-down of today's society. "That's precisely why I limit my days on the river to one or two per year," was Jeff's sprite response. As a guru of taking life at an easy pace, he then added that working slower might help too. "In fact," he concluded, "the adage I live by goes something like: If you don't like how slow I am going, you are really going to hate my other speed." We both chuckled, but I know what he was getting at.

One of Jeff's recurring themes has always been the nagging inconsistency he sees in the human race. On one hand mankind is capable of so much creativity, but on the other so much hateful destruction. I bring this up as an example of the many divergent directions our conversations can take. "Look at the history of the world," Jeff will say, "one segment of mankind will be killing, conquering, obliterating, and forcing their beliefs upon others, while those on the other side seem to be pre-occupied with doing the same thing. It just seems more logical to try to get along." Jeff believes that we are not much better these days, we just mask it differently. "Man just keeps finding more subtle ways to hate and better ways to destroy," he always concludes, "and eventually there won't be much left." We both agree that the measure of a man's character only has meaning when compared to the lowest common denominator of depravity. We also believe that the power of creativity takes a whole lot less energy in the long run than clinging to the power of darkness — and the rewards are much greater. From where we sit, it seems so obvious.

The five-strip butts were placed in separate piles and the equipment started up once again. The first one passed through was hollowed a bit too deeply; so Glenn backed off the cutter on the next strip, and it resulted in an acceptable cut. The procedure began with one acceptable stick, and then another. With a few minor exceptions, the hollowing process works the same as taper cutting; so this allows me to slip back into another period of reflection.

During the *Grand Gathering* on the Grand River in Fergus, Ontario, last May, I was able to talk to a few other five-strip advocates and we all agreed that there is a lively action associated with five-sided construction. Followers of Claude Krieder and Nat Uslan have made the same observation in bygone years. In fact, it was this feel that attracted Krieder to building five-strippers in the first place, and his enthusiasm was based upon the findings of the rod experimentalist Robert Crompton from the twenties. Uslan was also impressed with Crompton's knowledge of stress and tapers. Not only was the glue seam opposing one flat considered a structural advantage, but wider flats containing more power fibers separated by only five glue seams in total also made great structural sense. The fact that the interior walls were also wider, allowing for more gluing surface, was considered a positive as well.

I notice Wayne coming into the room while we are midway through the hollowing. He smiles when he sees the five-strippers. "They ain't natural," Wayne will usually say. Once stating that nothing in nature occurs in combinations of five, he couldn't figure why I would want to open the door to unforeseen headaches. In response to his insensitivity I set forth the example of a starfish while holding up my *five* fingers, but he just shook his head and stated, "Yea, along with the devil's pentacle." He had a point — or five of them. But then I replied, "Just think of the advertising gimmicks: 'A devil of a rod' or 'One helluva of casting tool.'" Wayne was thus amused with all the marketing possibilities.

Afterwards, I did some research. It seems that about four thousand years ago many people who dwelled in the country were known to be Nature worshippers, and since their lives were controlled by the whims of earthly events, being immersed in nature was a way of life for them. These country folks were also called pagans. In that culture the five-pointed star, termed a pentacle, developed as a symbol of the feminine side of humanity that was always seeking balance with the masculine side. It should be noted that the exact course of the planet Venus over an eight-year cycle traces a pentacle in the sky, and this fact thus explains the origins of the symbol as it relates to femininity. Furthermore, in Greek mythology Pan was the pastoral god of fertility where the five senses were revered amongst those who worshipped this odd looking satyr with goat horns, ears, and legs. It was only after Christianity came along expanding upon a one-God belief structure that pagan worshippers such as those who followed Pan and Nature were denounced. Elementary logic dictates how Christians used symbols of the pagans and transformed them into the images of the devil — right on down to the farmer's pitchfork. Originally the pentacle was a positive sign of life no more harmful than today's logo for our favorite football team. The pentacle, however, eventually got linked to the negative connotations associated with the devil in the development of Christian folklore.

Forms of pantheism once revered by pagans have evolved throughout the ages and still exist today. Hinduism is a prime example. More formally, these days it is a system that believes God or spirituality can be found within certain elements of the physical universe. Since the "boo boys" believe that you can find anything you want in the great temple of the outdoors, under this scenario maybe the five-strip rod is more closely allied to the forces of good than it is to the forces of evil. And since a bamboo rod could be considered a modern symbol of the natural world, the pent rod then makes great sense! "Give me five!" or "Five Alive!" may not be bad slogans for the pentagonal rod. I'll have to run these past Wayne — someday.

After Glenn touches the buttons to shut down the machines, silence descends upon the room just in time to catch the end of Wayne's statement, "…the public's heads are buried so deep in the sand that corporations get away with murder, and the government supports it!" You can understand why Wayne, being dead in the eyes of the government, could be sporting such an attitude. But then, I have a few pictures of prominent culprits responsible for corporate turmoil hanging on my wall just below the portrait of Alfred E. Newman I cut off a cover of the *Land's End* catalog a few years ago.

"It's a brave new world out there," I interjected, " we are now serving the god of Big Business and our politicians are their patron saints! Greece had their pagan gods and we have ours. The only problem is that a lot of these guys use the Bible to support this idolatry."

Pardon my sarcasm, but I am still a bit upset about a steelhead trip I made to the Klamath in September 2002. I had been sadly fishing the Klamath the year before at the exact moment the ghastly events were occurring on 9/11. To pay tribute to those folks who died so needlessly and to get back in touch with something I felt that I lost that day, I returned the next year for my own memorial service on the beautiful Klamath. Little did I realize that at that exact time in 2002 the president was shaking hands with Oregon farmers to cement a deal that would immediately divert flows from the Klamath to their fields. This whole affair is very well documented! The first of the 33,000 steelhead and salmon that eventually died because of this Administrative decision started to float by while I was standing in the river and casting a fly to a memory I'd like to forget. Such irony! And while it is true that this issue is more complex than it seems, no matter how it is sliced, the end result was a lot of dead fish. In the big picture, fish and the economy linked to them are always low on the totem pole of consideration.

We are free thinkers at the shop who evaluate all sides of every topic under the sun in lively and sometimes colorful debate. Before anyone jumps to conclusions, though, I would have to say that we are neither dyed-in-the-wool liberals nor stereotypical conservatives. That said, I would imagine if Rush Limbaugh ever sat in on one of our discussions, he'd be back on those painkillers in no time flat. When it comes to the politics of trout, we are unwavering — regardless as to what side of the political aisle one may sit on. Under the New World Order, those of us who care, and presumably that includes every one who fly fishes, are going to have to fight for every trout in the future.

"Anybody hear what's going on with the clean water legislation these days?" Jeff asked in reference to impending challenges to the act in congress.

"We don't need any changes there," was Glenn's emphatic reply. As a former fishery biologist, he is well aware of the benefits to the fisheries throughout the country that came about as a result of the Clean Water Act enacted by the Nixon Administration in 1972.

"Of the corporations, by the corporations, for the corporations," was my two-cents worth of commentary. "Unfortunately, the fly fishing corporation gets the leftovers."

As a company that makes its living off a clean environment, we have been dismayed of late as to the latitude given to the corporate entities when it comes to the deregulation that includes allowing companies to police themselves with regard to pollution issues. This is sort of like making income tax voluntary. Remember, these are the same guys responsible for the shenanigans and scandals that led to the loss of retirement accounts and nest eggs for millions of Americans to start off this century. Not exactly beacons of trust! And this should concern every serious minded angler as well. At a time when there is so much unrest around the world, it seems that behind the scenes, while we are not looking, deals are being made that are not necessarily fish friendly.

This is not to say that corporations and the environment can't coexist in harmony. In a lot of cases they do. "Balance and common ground are essential," Jeff will always say in any discussion.

There are great examples of cooperative efforts here in Montana as well as in other parts of the country.

Although this approach to complex problems can take much time and goodwill to resolve, the multi-lateral benefits to communities and local economies are immense. Montana needs its traditional businesses, but it also needs the new traditions that include fly fishing and tourism. We firmly believe that both can co-exist and flourish.

"In all honesty," Jeff skeptically piped up, concerned that the Orwellian Age was only a few decades late in arriving, " I fear we are drifting away from a government that is for the people and by the people. Instead of sitting down at a table and figuring these things out by committee, a lot of the decisions affecting our lives are being made by Big Brother and the boys."

"Yea, and we have way-y-y too much Big Brother," Glenn added. " What we need, from where I'm looking, is more Big Sister!"

"The problem is that no one thinks for themselves anymore," Wayne interjects in the free running exchange. " 'They'," making those parenthetical quotation marks with two fingers of each hand, "make you feel unpatriotic for even speaking out against the established party line anymore — whatever it is."

Then I told the story of a clergy friend who once stated to me that "God doesn't reward stupidity" in reference to the belief that somehow God will miraculously bail the human race out of all the bad situations man has created for himself. If that doesn't occur, then it is just as easy for mankind to blame or justify everything on whatever deity best suits its fancy. "In fact, if some folks could sue God, they would," he'd shake his head. My friend went on to say that much of what happens to the human race is of its own doing. If you make a decision or allow one to be made for you by not asking the right questions or evaluating the consequences, then bad things happen. In his estimation, that's why God gave us a brain.

"All the fly anglers I have ever met have well honed brains," I concluded, "we just need to be more relentless about speaking up on behalf of our rivers. We can no longer afford to stay quiet!"

I reflect a bit about my Dad. He was such a black-and-white, right-or-wrong, dogmatic sort of guy; so I think he would have had a bit of trouble with our above conversation. But with so many people on the planet these days, I know he understood how complicated life had become. Although he would regularly tolerate my outside-the-box viewpoints, we rarely discussed anything that mattered. It was a safe ground that we sought, but this is precisely the innocuous state of status quo with regard to important issues that insidious forces of power rely upon in the general public to slip through changes that benefit the few at the expense of the many. Right up to the end, Dad was a good soldier, and he never could understand why my brother and I would catch fish and not keep them.

And so goes another afternoon in the shop, one conversation after another. You may not agree, but your input is welcome. Questions and discussions, and there is never an answer. We live life the same way we build rods.

Instead of tomorrow, Glenn decides that the gluing will be done the day after. He has already gone to his bench where he will take the finished strips and carefully examine each one. This process takes quite a while. Any strip that isn't cut perfectly or shows a blemish of some sort will be set aside. The best will then be matched into several groups of six, assembled and taped together. The tape will subsequently be slit to lay open the six strips next to each other. The same will be done for the five strip butts. At that point the sections will be steel brushed to eliminate any excess fragments and finally trimmed to the same length. Then they are ready to glue. He will assemble the reject batch as well and mark them in red. We can use these blanks for prototypes, or just maybe a replacement section for an old clunker rod brought to the shop by some one who found it in his father's basement.

V

The word is that an Arctic blast will be descending into the area within two or three days. At least the *Weather Channel* says so. Thirty to forty degrees below zero temperatures are forecast for nighttime lows and, from past experience, I know the wind chill will be unbearable. Under these conditions townsfolk tend to hunker down in their houses — trying to stay warm and making sure that pipes don't freeze. Survival mode can be tense, especially if the cold lingers for days on end. It has been four years since this part of Montana has seen anything that resembles a normal winter. Explained as just one more symptom of climate warming, this part of the state seems to have fallen into a black hole impenetrable by the forces of nature. The best this region has been able to experience during this four-year period are moderately cold temperatures and a bit of snow here and there. This is a considerable change from the conditions responsible for the white capped peaks that Lewis and Clark reported on their trek through the area in August of 1804.

For a guy who loves winter, I feel cheated. Although skiing is something I left behind back in my youth and ice fishing has become more of a dalliance now than it was ten years ago, the winter is usually an inspirational time to get things done that have been left on the back burner for months on end. When the weather is really bad, it is easy to build a rod or write a story. On the other hand, when the temperatures stay above freezing it is just as easy to yield to the allure of casting away a day or two on a local tailwater. My will is weak when it comes to this seduction. The biggest problem associated with this void of winter weather is the corresponding lack of snowpack that comes back to haunt our rivers in the summer with very low and overheated flows. Not only does enthusiasm wane under these conditions, but the pang of conscience casting a fly to fish that are so vulnerable weighs heavily on my sense of propriety.

And because drought severely impacts the Big Hole, our town really feels the effects since it is a free flowing river with no dam. The lower stretch of this beautiful river flows below the second of the twin bridges outside of town about a mile. Under these circumstances there is usually not much water left by the time August rolls around. So at the sign of any bad weather looming on the horizon anytime between November and June, not only I, but everyone in town gets cautiously exuberant.

At this time of year, the Big Hole looks like an Alaskan ice highway, but with intermittent veins of open flowing water that should deter any sober soul from becoming too cavalier or reckless. Old timers once used long poles, a bobber, and a hook baited with maggots to reach out from the frozen ledges to fish these icy slots in the river for whitefish and the occasional trout. There was a time when I did the same thing using a fly rod and brightly colored flies, a method that met with varied success. In the winter whitefish don't have quite the same stigma as they do in the summer. Consequently, there is a certain amount of chic that goes along with toughing out the elements, if not the dangers, of fishing from the ledge. The four years of low snowpack, however, have translated into fewer trout and whitefish in this marginal section of water. Consequently, freezing one's butt off on a slick tongue of ice with little chance of finding a "whitie" — despite the proximity — doesn't seem quite so appealing under these circumstances.

When we do get adequate water for a few years in a row, though, this is a wonderful piece of home water, particularly during the spring or fall. There are never a lot of fish in this section, even under the best of conditions. But when the sweet scent of sticky sap fills the warm breezes of an early spring afternoon with a delightful fragrance, there are few excuses not to grab a rod, hang up the "gone fishing" sign and take a walk up or down from the bridge on the Big Hole. The water is usually a bit high and bronze in color, and a well placed woolly bugger normally produces something in an hour or two. Fishing in the golden glow of autumn can also be decent if the flows have been maintained throughout the summer. Hanging on the wall of my mind is the beautiful huge male brown caught during the very first season of fall fishing this home stretch of water. I have been trying to catch that fish again ever since.

Drought plans enacted by the Big Hole Watershed Committee the past few years have mitigated the negative impacts of low flows by creatively working with ranchers to keep more water in the river. This effort does help stabilize the modest fish populations in our local water. Because the four of us value these days on the Big Hole, we regularly donate rods to Trout Unlimited to protect and enhance the dreams we chase. Tonight I sit and reflect upon those special fish from the past, pray for snow, and read letters from Lew Stoner written many years ago.

It is hard to believe that Lew Stoner and Robert Winther could have started the Winston Rod company during the ignominious year of 1929. It is even more difficult to comprehend that the company could have survived the Depression, and, subsequently, World War

A Wisp in the Wind

II. Whereas Winther had to bow out in the thirties because of financial considerations, Stoner plugged along with another partner Red Loskot until 1953. The fact that none of these guys were disciples of the East Coast bamboo tradition made the success of the company even more impressive. Seventy-five years later, the company and its viable bamboo "division" still chugs along with a spirit that is truly a credit to the history of cane in this country.

Stoner not only worked long hours to laboriously make rods, he obviously spent many more hours writing voluminous letters to prospective customers as a part of the service he felt the business required to seal the deal. He would write about rod actions, casting styles, line recommendations in addition to exchanging fishing stories. Much of what he talked about was the Winston ideology of bamboo construction along with trying to convince the public that the company built more than just distance casting and steelhead rods. He was primarily concerned with performance, although quality craftsmanship was a given in his mind. This was his livelihood, and there were many references to difficult times in his epistles.

In March of 1942 he writes: "I am in difficult spot, as to rods. With one restriction after another (due to wartime), I don't know that I can keep going, even alone as I am here now. And the overhead is high. To keep an entire plant set up, and make but a few rods, is to fail to earn even small wages above that overhead." In April 1949 he writes of a different problem. "You'll find them (rod builders) everywhere. Right now, you can find almost as many new rod "factories", too. As after War #1, they are a dime a dozen." He went on to add: "And history will repeat itself. Only two classes can survive, those who make a rod cheaper and consequently worse than all others, and those who can get at the top as to quality, and stay there. To some, (cheap) price is the biggest consideration in buying a rod or any other thing. Others, want the best. In the long run, the proof of time and use, and the clientele served, prove what is really the best." Another letter from 1950 reflects his concern with the proliferation of glass, steel, and beryllium/bronze rods. As a result: "We have not done too much business this year, but have much widened our field. We have opened a good deal in Europe...."

Stoner was certainly a contemporary more of both my grandfathers than he was with my father, but the sheer struggle just to exist evident in Stoner's letters gives insight to all the stories I have heard from my father about when he was growing up. Hardened by a reality I will never fully appreciate, it was no wonder that the way we both approached life were two worlds apart. Just like Stoner, both of my grandfathers along with my father were diligent with their hands. In those days, they had to be! But thanks to the fact that my father committed to a one-job career after World War II until his retirement, I was given the opportunity to choose from many paths — including the offbeat one that led to the trail left behind by Lew Stoner. To Stoner's credit, he stuck to a creative vision that helped him survive an era of economic devastation with a career of dignity.

Getting back to Pirsig's pressing problem with regard to romance and technology, as stated before, he was obsessed with finding that realm of commonality where the essence of both worlds overlapped. He concluded that the common ground was a third entity he called Quality — with a capital Q. But what is Quality, he would ask. He postulated that it is a property of both performance and appearance that can be recognized, but not necessarily defined. Although Pirsig was talking about Quality in more metaphysical terms, a study of how the bamboo rod evolved throughout the history of Winston from Stoner to Brackett would give about as much insight into the concept of Quality from every angle as Pirsig could have ever imagined. Whereas he eventually used the motorcycle to explain his abstract quandary, he could just as easily have used a bamboo rod.

On April 4, 1949 Stoner wrote a paragraph to a Mr. Helff that could best sum up the history of the company he started the year of the great stock market crash:

"In rods, there was a time when Leonard was an undisputed leader. He died, his graceless son took over, and Payne and Thomas and all the other good men jumped out and went into business on their own. They made the best rods on earth, and kept on making them. Their trouble was, that the world kept on moving, and they didn't! They are still making the same old rods. We, on the other hand, put just as much time improving rods, ways, means, methods, as in actual manufacture. Much of it goes out in the garbage, but a little of it proves itself. Nothing is ever so good that it can't be made better, and no one has a better chance to make it better than one who never ceases trying to, and who has all the background of years of that."

I don't know when Glenn would have read this excerpt, but I am convinced that the only reason the Winston bamboo fly rod still exists is because of Glenn's devoted dedication to Stoner's philosophy. He will tell stories of visiting the old shop in San Francisco with his grandfather in the fifties that sound more like trips to a land of enchantment. The shop was in a rough part of town, but throughout all the years of its existence, it was never robbed or burglarized. Glenn always figured that no one in that neighborhood would ever be able to figure out what to do with a fly rod even if they did steal it; thus, no one tried. If there was ever a person called to make bamboo rods, Glenn has to be the "Chosen One." And I believe

74

the San Francisco atmosphere is the same one Glenn has tried to emulate in our little shop in Twin Bridges. So far we have never had a rod stolen either, nor have we ever lost one.

For Glenn, rod building is just as much about appearance as it is about performance, but, ultimately, it is more about how these elements fit the fishing experience and entwine with the spirit of the people who have made Winston what it is. Whether it be the employees who have worked at the company throughout the years or the many folks who have come through the doors just to say hello, the rods only have significance in the context of people who appreciate what it is that we are creating. Like the old conundrum *if a tree falls in the forest does it make a sound if there is no one to hear it,* one might ask *does a bamboo rod really exist if there is no one on a river casting it.*

Visitors include artists, writers, rod builders, rod collectors and aficionados as well as those interested in learning about bamboo or even buying one. Many of these folks have become our friends. Like Stoner, Glenn will spend hours with prospective customers to help them choose a rod that fits their spirit, because, as we have discussed, the "bamboo way" is a calling of many dimensions. "Every serious angler ought to treat themselves to a bamboo of some sort at one point in their lives," Glenn will muse wistfully. Understanding the history, romance, and all the other intangibles that go into seventy-five years worth of building is perhaps the most important aspect of procuring one of our rods.

Every rod has a story, and we have heard many. Our files document some, but far too many have faded from our collective memories. Now and then, someone will call with a serial number and an accompanying tale of how a particular rod got into his or her hands. Our rods have gone to royalty, heads-of-state, other prominent individuals as well as to anglers from all walks of life, or to someone's grandfather. When we all got a chance to hold one with the name Bing Crosby once inscribed upon it by Doug Merrick we were each able to feel the extraordinary history still vibrating through the heart of the antique. It is an honor to be a part of this unfolding story, but the saddest chapter, as far as Glenn is concerned, is about the rods that have never been used.

Last summer Glenn received this Email, and he was delighted after reading it.

Dear Glenn and Jeff,

I am a bit awed addressing my parents, but my excitement is overflowing.I am rod #3185 purchased by a pleasant enough senior type fly angler in September 1997. He wanted to get a fine cane rod to pass on to his son. He was most thrilled when I arrived fresh and new, and he got me a fine Orvis CFO III reel. But he was so taken by my beautiful svelte figure that he almost never fished me — being afraid I might suffer injury.

Last week he spoke glowingly of me to another popular cane rod builder. My owner was told bluntly, but kindly, that you two would be most upset if you knew how I was being isolated and protected instead of being fished and enjoyed. Anyway, this morning my guy turned over a new leaf. He swears so. He fished me and seemed surprised at how much fun I was. He cast me with ease both far and fine. And best of all, he landed and released six chunky browns averaging sixteen inches. Of course, I didn't break. I didn't chip. I didn't take a set. I think, finally, I really have him hooked. My life in solitary darkness is ended.

*I just thought you would like to know how I am doing.
By the way, my boss says, "Thanks."*

Tight lines, finally, #3185 (Ford Swigart)

Glenn insists that our rods make sense only if they are
fished. But he also realizes that many buyers are collectors
who put the rod away to be unveiled once again at a much
later date. Every time we get a chance to see a "new rod"
that was placed into a closet years ago, we appreciate the
fact that someone did set it aside for posterity's sake. When
an unused Stoner rod from 1933 came into our hands a
few years back, it felt like we had just found the lost
treasure of the Sierra Madre. Another guy stopped by the
shop at one point with sixty or so *South Bend* and *Granger*
rods that he discovered tucked away in an old warehouse
he had just purchased in the Midwest. Since none of them
had ever been out of the tube, we felt like kids on the day
before Christmas sneaking a peak at this unusual bounty.

Glenn also asserts that bamboo rods are much more
durable than most folks think. He will often tell the story
of the time he and a friend were canoeing the Big Hole
under less than ideal conditions during a period of high
water in late June. At a point where the river split into
three braids, it was their misfortune to choose the wrong
channel. The constricted flow took control of the
aluminum craft like a demonic force, and with little time
to make an adjustment the canoe "T-boned" on a
protruding log in the middle of the channel. It bent around
the snag like a tight-fitting glove. Since saving themselves
was a priority, rescuing the equipment on board, which
included two graphite rods and one bamboo, was out of
the question. Everything spilled into the roaring river.

It took a few days to devise a strategy to recover the crumpled canoe, but the rest of the equipment would have to wait until the water receded with the approach of July. With a bit of good fortune the rods, or what was left of them, were finally recovered from a deeper hole a few weeks later, just a couple hundred yards down river from the mishap. The graphite rods were shredded strands of carbon fibers with battered reels still attached, a testimony to the sheer power of rapidly flowing water. Although the Winston bamboo was well rounded on the corners, it was completely intact — and fishable.

When I showed up at the shop the afternoon of the day between making the last cuts and gluing the batch of assembled strips, Glenn had completed preparing the blanks for tomorrow's venture and was putting them into storage. Sitka made his position known. After a short greeting and sharing a few insights from the Stoner letters, I headed to my work area. There was a folder on the bench with a letter from a physician in Mississippi and a photo of the rod he had just completed under the long distance tutelage of Glenn. It looked very nice, and the builder was obviously tickled and grateful for the support. I had just gotten a snapshot, which I stuck to the wall, of a seven piece casting rod we recently refinished for a local fellow from Sheridan. Since it was once his father's, he enclosed it in a shadow box to be displayed above his mantle. On the adjacent cabinet was a letter from another appreciative fellow who won a rod as a grand prize at our Trout Unlimited Bar-B-Que a few years back.

Since Glenn has an errand to run, he bids ado and then departs.

Standing on my bench are six rods that need finishing touches for the upcoming show circuit. There are also several five-strip prototypes I like to shake now and then. The six foot three-incher is for my friend Dave Slaughter who prefers little headwater streams filled with small cutthroat and brook trout. He recently sent me one of his beautiful hand-carved creations, a golden trout that now adorns the top of my bookcase at home. I hope the little five-sider will be a fitting gesture of thanks. Then there is the broken quad staring me in the face that snapped while casting on a windy Missouri River day in October. At the time I didn't think much of the soft-sided cooler containing a six-pack of Missoula's own *Moose Drool* that fell off a shelf and was lying oddly next to my strung up four-sided rod placed gently on the cushioned sleeping bag in the back of the pick-up. But I was cursing those beers as the butt section popped and then flopped in the breeze while casting to several sipping eighteen-inch rainbows. Although bamboo rods are tough, surviving a direct hit by a cooler is probably expecting a bit too much. It wasn't a total loss. Since the beer didn't break, those *Moose Drools* helped drown my sorrows.

As Jeff comes in from lunch, he stops by to say hello and inserts the Nitty Gritty Dirt Band into the nearby tape player. "Did you see the paper this morning?" I asked.

"Not yet. What's up now?"

"The move is on to repeal the ban on the use of cyanide again."

Jeff shakes his head as he walks to his bench. I hate to make it seem that the "boo boys" are just a bunch of "pissers and moaners," but the cyanide issue in this state is serious business — and a touchy subject. In modern gold mining, a cyanide solution is used to leach small quantities of gold from excavated ore, leaving behind very acidic piles of rocks contaminated with released heavy metals. This cyanide mixture is stored in open ponds lined with plastic that often leak as well. The track record of this type of mining has been less than stellar, leaving in its wake acidic streams and polluted drinking water. On several occasions the companies responsible for these atrocities have walked away from any accountability, thereby sticking the American taxpayer with the bill to clean up their mess. Consequently, the citizens of Montana voted to make this type of procedure illegal a few years back, but big business proponents keep trying to undo the deal. In Jeff's case there is heap leach operation just above his property. With gold prices on the rise, the colossal mine proposed for the upper Blackfoot River is now back into the picture. Lest we forget, the Clark Fork River outside of Butte remains the ever-present monument to those concerned about the need for more responsible mining practices in this state.

"I hate to come out always looking like the bad guy," says Jeff, " because, in all truth, there should be mining in Montana. But it just can't jeopardize the health, welfare, and economic opportunities for the rest of us. What is gained if some people make money but destroy the quality of life for everyone else in the process?"

Frankly, the "boo boys" get bent out of shape with the radio talk show propaganda that labels those of us committed to the environment as nothing more than liberal obstructionists. Only simpletons could make such statements. These issues go far beyond tree-huggers and Bambi lovers, and sound science dictates that if we love our children, then the environment should not be a political soccer ball in a game that determines the outcome of their futures. As far as we are concerned *Thou shalt not screw the environment* should be the unequivocal Eleventh Commandment. With so little fresh water available to a growing population around the planet, it would seem that taking care of what we have left would fall under the category of supreme urgency. *If one hand is cleaning the toilet where has the other been that's holding the sandwich?* A bit of Zen for the modern ages!

The back door jingles, and in comes Wayne for a bit of respite after struggling all morning with a ferruling problem on a rod at his shop. When the obligatory "How's it going?" is taken care of, we all start chatting back and forth. Eventually, Wayne works his way over to my bench where we share a few one-liners about the five-sided rods standing there. It doesn't take long before Wayne is updating me on today's headache in the world of rod building, when somehow the conversation turns to catfish and the days of his youth growing up in eastern Nebraska. Topics in our on-going discussions change with more regularity than a Las Vegas chorus line. My mind then drifted to the forty-pound flathead catfish swimming around the super aquarium in *Cabela's* of Mitchell, South Dakota. On a past visit gigantic Gerald swam from under its log and meandered up to the clear wall holding the contents of his home together. After staring longingly at me for a few minutes through the glass with its expressively drooping "Fu Manchu", the Goliath then returned directly to its lair. I could only imagine that landing this brute on any kind of gear would be like dragging in four bowling balls — still in their carrying bags.

"On my 'to do' list in the future is some serious catfishing," I blurt, realizing that this would require going in a direction that is one-hundred and eighty degrees from trout and about that many degrees in temperature and humidity combined.

"You'll love the way we fished for them," Wayne laughs tipping the brim of his hat.

As a budding Tom Sawyer, he was enthralled with the stories of his father and the escapades of town locals who had nicknames like Heavy Grinder, Fat Petrie, and Shammy. To hear Wayne tell it, one sultry summer day Heavy Grinder and the boys took it upon themselves to pass on to Wayne and his buddies the fine art of snatching catfish from under logs in the local river. According to Wayne, it took a lot of practice to get the timing just right.

"You had to wait for an extremely hot day since that would slow the fish down considerably, and then you'd carefully feel for them under any hiding spot like a log, brush pile, or overhanging clump. When you really got good at it you brought your forearm tight behind its dorsal just at the same time you stuck your other hand down its throat far enough to pop the air bladder. You had to be careful not to get stung by the sharp projectile on its fins. That hurt like hell! Done right, though, the cat would belly up immediately, and then it was ready for the gunny sack."

He continues. "One day Heavy Grinder got his big arm stuck in the mouth of a huge cat that scraped him bad. He never got the fish, but after that he always showed the scars on his forearm where the gouges got terribly infected."

That made me think about wrestling a fish about the size of Gerald. I cringe.

"Yep. When you grow up in Nebraska, fun was as hard to come by as an unmarried Mormon." He went on with stories about retrieving a set line at night in a tornado and dropping M-80 firecrackers through holes in the ice so that Heavy Grinder and the boys could spear the stampeding fish at a trench they cut in the ice further down river.

"Heck, we were kids," Wayne shrugs. "What did we know?" Reminiscing, perhaps, about long departed relatives, he concludes, "Those were the days, though. You know, family and all."

Jeff then asks Wayne, "Selling any rods lately?"

"Eh, just one. It's slow out there," Wayne answers, volunteering the observation.

"Not like the days after *A River Runs Through It*," Jeff inserts with some thought. "What we had to sell back then blended so nicely with the romantic portrayal of fly fishing as an inspirational way of life."

"Everything the movie started in the nineties seems to have definitely come to an end on 9/11," I add. "Since fly fishing is a feel-good pursuit, the nineties' enthusiasm has been totally stifled in the depressing aftermath of a nation's not feeling too good about life in the dawning age of terrorism."

"Ironically," Wayne reflects, "if there is one thing that could help folks feel better, it is fly fishing."

"True," Jeff replies while fidgeting with something on his bench. "Maybe it is up to those of us in the business to nurture this idea."

"From a marketing standpoint," I respond, "that's still the message we need to get out there." I ponder again. "More importantly, that's the message we need to get out there for the health of everyone on the planet."

"And bamboo rods connect all these intangibles together so nicely," says Jeff. "Sometimes I think that's why folks buy our rods."

"Yea," Wayne interjects in his typical pragmatic fashion, "but that's a tough notion to sell."

"It is," I acknowledge, "and it would be a shame to trivialize the concept by trying to market it. In that regard though, a lot of the guys trying to make a living selling rods in this economy have to work just as hard marketing as they do building. It's not much different than Stoner's time. I imagine Per Brandin, Mike Clark, Bob Sommers and a few of the other established names have waiting lists, but it is quite a chore for other good builders to get their creations out to the public when all they really want to do is build."

Wayne admits that he will have to make more of an effort with respect to this aspect of the business once his unique rods are to the point that he is satisfied. Of course, for some craftsmen, being satisfied is an ever-elusive goal.

"I'd like to think that we are promoting an enjoyable time that is as fun as it is meaningful," concludes Jeff as he gathers his belongings and heads for the door spouting one last thought. "And, hopefully, what we do create is a beautiful tool that helps someone experience nirvana while standing knee-deep in a river."

"Now that would be a tool worth buying," I say as Jeff leaves and Wayne soon follows.

"See you at gluing?" I ask Wayne in a rhetorical tone.

"As long as we don't have to do any of those crazy five-strippers," he says with a sly smile.

I finish the day at my bench thinking back upon the year in lugubrious solitude.

VI

The Grand River, which flows through Fergus, Ontario, is distinct because it has been resurrected from the trash heap of degraded rivers common to areas of heavy population inspired by a united vision as to what a revitalized river could mean to the health and psyche of a community. The section running through town is cool and clear thanks to a bottom release dam above Fergus that impounds the water known as Belwood Lake. In the early nineties several community and agency leaders from around the area devised a plan to clean up the river and provide guaranteed flows that would support trout. After a multi-year catch-and-release program of stocking, the Grand has become a model for reclaimed rivers that could be used throughout North America.

The river now sustains a very nice population of brown trout supported by a prolific array of hatches. Folks from around the East visit Fergus and the neighboring town of Elora just to cast a fly for challenging trout of all sizes, thereby generating regular tourist dollars into the local economy. Also, the neighborhoods through which the river flows would rather deal with anglers and healthy water than the ugly alternative; consequently, everybody wins in this scenario. It is on the bank of this renovated waterway that every two years the *Grand Gathering* takes place in a beautiful park by the dam. This get-together includes bamboo rod builders from Canada and the United States as well as those folks who are just interested in learning more about cane. These types of gatherings have been occurring more and more throughout both countries the past decade as a testimony to the growing interest in bamboo, and they are also great places to meet some very fine folks.

It was my pleasure to be a part of this group last May, and the night before the festivities began I met up with a guide from the local fly shop and Ohio based builder Jeff Wagoner to try our luck on the Grand. The sky was a pewter colored curtain when we all met at a local access, and the cool air mass that had descended upon the region during the afternoon discouraged any chance for surface activity. Despite the conditions, our guide friend Paul took us to one of his favorite spots on the river just as the skies opened up and heavy rain began to fall. Even through the extreme wetness and oppressive gloom, the evening was peaceful and still. But if it wasn't for those few big noses that occasionally popped out through the dark slick of a long tailout, we surely would have been back to the wooden barn used for community functions and drinking the first scotch of the weekend much sooner than we did get there. I enjoyed getting to know Jeff because he was a kindred soul who had expressed an interest in working at Winston years ago. Glenn has regularly communicated with him since that time. Under Paul's direction we both swung wet flies through the lengthy pool in the descending grayness of a late evening thick with moisture. At one point I noticed two silhouettes on the bridge behind us waving in our direction. It was author Kathy Scott and her rod building husband David Van Burgel. They had just arrived from Maine. It figured, they later said, that the only two guys foolish enough to be out under such conditions would be Jeff and me. "Just testing to see if our rods get waterlogged," I would retort. Eventually, Jeff and I each hooked a nice brown on the kind of evening that if I could click my heels and return to that exact moment in time, I would not hesitate.

Why I fish a bamboo rod can be summed up in experiences like this one on the Grand. John Gierach's book *Fishing Bamboo* starts with a quote from John Irving: "When you love something, you have the capacity to bore everyone about *why* — it doesn't matter why." Yet the one fascinating property of the human intellect is its compelling drive to understand *why*, and, equally, the need to explain *why*. Author Robert Pirsig was consumed with this desire. The frustrating aspect, however, of the simple question *why* is that there is rarely a satisfactory answer unless it is in the realm of cause and effect. Getting a good handle on *why* is like trying to catch a gust of wind in a bucket; and even if you do, it would be difficult to prove that it is there. So when someone asks *why is casting bamboo better than any other material* or *why should anyone even think about fishing bamboo,* the ability to discuss the subject makes good sense only because the *why* is usually discovered somewhere between the lines of the conversation.

For me, *why bamboo* is best talked about in the context of a "bamboo kind of day." Since it is my business to know graphite rods as a part of my duty at Winston, I don't always fish with a bamboo. On the other hand, I am always looking for a bamboo kind of day. This is a self-imposed criterion when I intuitively know that the preconditions of weather, river, and fishing partner will blend into a perfect combination for using my favorite cane rod. On these occasions the spirit of fly fishing often merges with the essence of art, function, and friendship, and when all these factors do come together, usually wonderful things happen. Pirsig would likely identify this level of experiencing reality as the third entity he calls Quality. This is the realm where nuts and bolts, art and romance, heart and soul all meld to create an intangible state of meaning and value that transcend the mundane. For me, simply stated, this is why bamboo.

This past June my brother and I took a pair of small rods to a little stream we like to visit in Western New York. Throughout the evening the sky spit a few raindrops as the smells of an early summer intensified in the humidity of an approaching thunderstorm. A few warblers reveled in the willows while a wood thrush echoed like a bell in an empty room. We fished the canopied creek draped with lush hardwoods. Captivated by the cream-colored green drake spinners that modest sized trout would gobble with enthusiasm, we cast our flies to those same browns with the hope that they would come up just one more time. As we walked back from the creek in total darkness the rain began to descend more steadily, and at the vehicle we quietly talked about the declining health of our father in solemn conclusion to a bamboo kind of day.

Again, in September the smoke from another forest fire-filled summer finally gave way to a series of crisp, cool days with Big Sky blue touching the juniper speckled hills of orange tinged outcroppings in sharp tones that had been muted for two months. As the mid-morning sun cast long shadows through the illuminated leaves of yellow, the building warmth of day common in early fall steadily replaced the frosty air that had accumulated throughout the evening past. I had hoped to find a few fish up on "tricos" in the spring creek-like flow that was mostly ground water recharge from a year of heavy irrigation, but there were no bugs to be found. A glimpse into the crystalline pools, though, revealed many more brown trout than I expected to see — some nice ones, too, queued nose to tail for several yards. They looked to be asleep. I brought the four-sided rod this day because it is a good hopper tool, and the hoppers were still active. After tying on a small pattern, the first cast inspired an explosion of activity. The dormant appearing trout shed their lethargic body language and individuals from the line-up erupted in a competitive rush to be the first to sample the inducement. For the next hour many fish rose to my hopper with reckless abandon throughout a consecutive series of runs.

I chose this particular day to pay tribute to the young daughter of a longtime friend who had recently succumbed to leukemia, and it couldn't have been more serene. While I landed another brilliantly dressed brown it came to me that the richness of our existence depends upon how we handle issues of mortality. Along the edge of the stream, I found a blooming Rocky Mountain Aster. In her memory I placed this small violet flower upon the resplendent ribbon of clarity. I then thought about the young soldier in Iraq who had written a letter to the editor of *Fly Fisherman* longing for the day he would be able to cast a fly once again. It made me sad. He reminded me of another friend who became a consummate steelheader after his mother sent him books about this magnificent fish while he was serving in Viet Nam. My friend believed that steelhead saved his spirit, and, ultimately, his life from descent into depression. Before leaving this bamboo kind of day behind I caught another trout and dedicated it to that boy serving somewhere in Iraq.

I can hardly discuss a bamboo kind of day without mentioning the significance of a totem fish. Throughout the career of any angler there exists the memory of one fish, or possibly more, which represents a symbolic catalyst to an experience that defies words to describe it. In fact, the very thought of this fish can trigger a flashback to that exact moment in time many years afterwards in such a manner that the very remembrance of the occasion can offer a refreshing present day retreat for the mind. For me, there are about seven fish that stand out, and if I stood them on top of one another they would create a totem pole of meaningful memories. Understandably, totem fish come along only once in a while — but that's what makes them so special.

After the *Grand Gathering* had concluded, my good friend Carl O' Conner from Toronto offered to take me to one of his favorite places in Ontario. The Saugeen River is in the Lake Huron drainage, and it is a difficult river to access. Carl's friend, however, lives near the upper river, and his property provides a pathway to the water. The lower Saugeen is renown for prolific runs of Lake Huron steelhead, but this upper section is more noted for its populations of wild brown trout. Both Carl and his friend Wilhelm have rehabilitated some spring seeps along the river that now serve as little spawning feeders to this particular section of the Saugeen. They are both proud of their efforts, and this hard work has been rewarded over the years with some very nice trout caught throughout the water that flows adjacent to Wilhelm's property. Carl was anxious to share a morning on this particular piece of meaningful water.

A few years beforehand Carl extended this same invitation to both my brother and me, but that day the temperature pushed a very uncomfortable one hundred degrees. In fact, it was a record high for the date. This was in sharp contrast to the previous November, when Rick and I spent a frigid day attempting to catch steelhead on the Saugeen near Walkerton. Although the thermometer never got out of the teens, it was the wind that really got to us. By the end of the afternoon, the folks at the neighborhood *Tim Horton's* knew us by name, since we took a coffee break every hour. When it comes to the Saugeen, the conditions commonly conspire against us, and the experience always ends with a Canada goose chase kind-of-tale that never has anything to do with catching a fish.

When Carl and I arrived at Wilhelm's, he and his wife Ann had dinner waiting. Their rustic home looked more like an Atlantic salmon lodge, with all the appropriate flies and memorabilia that reflected Wilhelm's passion for this spirited fish. As I learned at the table, both of them were anxiously anticipating the day within a few years when they would be able to retire to this remote part of lower Ontario. After the meal, Wilhelm took us on a walk around his property bordered by a northern forest of conifers and birch. He showed us his garden and the work he was doing on a spring-fed pond for brook trout. Upon returning to his home, he picked up a vase in the living room jammed with many sticks cut from the branches of local streamside willows. Wilhelm explained that each represented the exact length of an individual brown trout he had caught and released over the years in the section of the river below his house. Since some of the sticks were over twenty-one inches, it was difficult not to get excited.

But, of course, this was the Saugeen, and the memory of past experiences snapped me back to reality quickly.

We awoke the next morning to a heavy fog caused by a period of light showers throughout the night. Since Wilhelm and his wife were scheduled to return to Toronto by mid morning, he could only offer a few tips about his home water as well as provide me with one of his favorite flies for fishing this section of the Saugeen. It was a beautiful classic-style wet leadwing coachman tied by Wilhelm himself. After thanking him for the fly and their hospitality, his only request was that I write a paragraph in his guest log after our time on the water.

Upon saying good-bye, Carl and I headed down to the river just as the sun began to melt the fog with radiant fingers of light. The first view of the Saugeen looked more like a postcard from Montana. The river, illuminated by columns of broken sunshine, featured a slightly tannic colored flow moving through a series of riffles, runs and tailouts. As we strung up the rods alongside the water an occasional light Hendrickson would float by, but we noticed that no fish showed any interest. Although the river was too high to be fordable, there was a wide range of water available on our side; so Carl headed upstream and I meandered into the pool at the base of the path. That morning I fished one of Wayne's snappy five-weights that he lent to me for testing. Since his rod is designed to easily deliver a long line, I was definitely able to cover a good portion of the run all the way to the other side.

The first pass through this very appealing stretch produced no action on a floating Hendrickson pattern. After I methodically worked the run again with a woolly bugger, another hour had passed. It was an absorbing morning filled with delightful earthly scents, and I was just excited to be able to fish the Saugeen under such ideal conditions. In fact, as the time unfolded I got caught up in one of those Atlantic salmon moments when just swinging a fly was enchanting enough. After the second pass was completed I decided to search out new water, but not before trying the head of the pool with Wilhelm's coachmen. After replacing the woolly bugger, I noticed Carl working his way toward me just as I was stepping back into the run.

The first cast with the wet fly stretched out to the midpoint of the river. The second was a bit further. The third landed in a subtle edge off a break on the other side. Then it was cast, swing, step, pick-up, and cast again. About halfway through the run I saw a swirl just as the fly landed on the other side, and when the line tightened it elicited the same exuberance one gets when hooking a salmon. The fish was strong, and it fought well on Wayne's lightweight eight-footer. Carl arrived just as I was landing the eighteen-incher. Although a fish of this size isn't uncommon in Montana, an angler must be able to appreciate a fish within the context of where it is caught. After all, this was the Saugeen. Carl was as excited as I was, and he couldn't wait to take a snapshot of the butter colored beauty. Even as I write this I am taken back to that moment — a wonderful day, rod, river, friend, and trout all rolled into one. A totem fish caught on a bamboo kind of day.

Since Carl and I decided to try another stream in the afternoon, we left the Saugeen as the sun rose prominently in the noon sky. Before our departure, however, I fulfilled my promise to make an entry in Wilhelm's log, detailing my history with the Saugeen and the thrill of catching one of its unique brown trout. I concluded the passage with the statement that "I hoped the fish was stick-worthy." And as I closed the book, I placed upon the page a willow branch Carl had cut to the exact length of the trout that we had just released.

VII

Today we glue. This is as much a social event as it is work. The time usually glides by on the wings of animated conversation, and this activity provides the best opportunity for visitors to observe and ask any question that comes to mind about building rods or favorite fishing spots or politics *de jour.* You bring it up and we can talk about it for hours.

First, there is the preparation. The room is rearranged with a bench for applying the glue placed in the middle of the only open space on the floor next to the milling machine. Upon this bench glue will be applied to the exposed interior of the six taped-together strips. Of course, there are the five-strippers that will be done as well. Since I added the five-strip sections I had already cut with the handmill that were on my bench to the strips we milled the other day, there will be forty sections to assemble today. That's a lot of gluing considering that we usually do twenty-five or fewer. Glenn has neatly stood the taped sections against the counter next to the application bench. While I mix the glue, Wayne sets up the binding machine on the far wall perpendicular to Glenn's workspace. Since this is a difficult machine to explain, just know that it is a system of drive wheels hand spun by Wayne. A drive belt rotates the blank through a plastic tube while a separate spool of string attached to the section by a half-hitch spirals around the total length of the glued strips to bind them tightly. After one pass the section is spun through again with the string going in the opposite direction, and this gives the blank a criss-crossed pattern of closely wrapped bindings along the entire piece.

While Wayne puts the finishing touches to the binder, Glenn places a long board on top of his workspace. After washing the excess glue off the blank that comes out of the binding machine, he will lay the bound section upon the board and work each strip into a seated position so that it is aligned dead straight with the other strips. Only when Glenn is satisfied does he hang the blank in the drying cabinet with a weight suspended from the bottom end to keep it plumb. The weights will be removed in a few days and then the pieces will need several more months to cure. As the three of us tend to this process, Jeff is in his cubicle removing the string from an old blank that we glued last year. With that completed, he will then begin to scrape and sand the section as the first step of building a finished rod. Because our hands will be quite sticky, it is also Jeff's duty to make sure that the music plays all day.

After I mix the catalyst into the specially formulated white glue, it is poured through a sieve into a container so that a brush can be used to apply the adhesive to the blanks. Although the glue is a low-toxic, water-soluble product, it is impermeable to wetness after it is dry. After slopping a generous amount of glue onto three or four separate sections, I begin to roll each into a six-sided blank, wrap rubber bands around the ends, remove the tape, and then hand them one by one to Wayne, as needed. It takes five to ten minutes to bind each blank; that is, if there are no problems. So it goes, the process continues until everything is finished. But just as the four of us begin to banter back and forth, the bell on the back door jingles and one of our neighbors walks through the door.

Bixx is a fly fisherman who moved to the area in the eighties. An entrepreneur with many talents, he has had to use all of them to raise a family in the economically depressed state of Montana. As a hobby, Bixx loves to find unusual items at flea markets and second hand stores throughout the West and auction them on the Internet. Surprisingly, he still finds an occasional bamboo rod that has some value. Today he wanted to update Jeff and Glenn about a rod they both had put on *eBay* to raise money for a friend of Jeff's who was dealing with a serious illness in the family. Bixx was handling the transaction.

Whenever possible at the shop, we try to support community efforts. Whether it is the Day Care, the Library, Trout Unlimited, or a family ravaged by sickness, we donate our time and effort to try to make a difference. In this case, Glenn and Jeff combined to make a five-piece pack rod with glass ferrules, and apparently the bidding was going quite well. We were excited. Before running off to another project, Bixx filled us in on some of his fall fishing escapades. While we were thanking him as he said good-bye, another blank rolled through the binder.

It wasn't long before the doorbell chimed once again, and a recently retired fellow who had just moved to Twin Bridges entered the room. Dave just wanted to spend a bit of time watching and chatting while we were tending to our duty. We each took turns giving Dave a brief synopsis of what we were doing, and then the conversation shifted to the Jefferson River.

Of all the folks who have recently moved to southwestern Montana, Dave seemed to be one of the few who is truly concerned about the plight of the river. After being ravaged by four years of drought, it has taken a monumental effort on the part of the local Trout Unlimited chapter working with the Jefferson Watershed Council to keep the river from drying up once again like it did in 1988. Additionally, Dave couldn't help but notice the serious decline in fish populations over the few years that he has been here.

"And what are they going to do about the lack of water in the Clark Canyon Reservoir?" Dave asked.

By 2003 the reservoir was drawn down to an all-time low, mostly because of a poor winter snowpack, but also because of water mismanagement throughout this period of dryness. The Beaverhead River feels the direct impact, since it directly flows out of the reservoir. After the Beaverhead meets the Ruby River above Twin Bridges, it then converges with the Big Hole below town to form the Jefferson. Since "the Jeff" obviously gets the leftovers of these three tributaries, there has been very little water remaining in either throughout the period of drought.

"There's not much anyone can do until it snows — a lot!" I stated. "Fortunately, watershed groups on all four rivers have been working cooperatively with irrigators to squeeze as much water into the rivers as possible to save the dwindling trout populations."

"How come the outfitting industry doesn't get more involved?" Dave asked again.

"Good question," Jeff replied sardonically.

"They have been spending the past several years trying not to be squeezed off the water by citizens who think the guides are responsible for overcrowding the rivers," Wayne says.

This issue has gotten rather contentious, and it is not going to go away. There is a contingent of Montanans who do not like the commercial usage of the rivers. There are others who wish non-residents would stay away too. Ironically, many of these folks spend little time working with groups to protect the resource; all they want to do is use it.

"While everyone is arguing who should and should not be on the water," Glenn inserts, "the rivers are drying up, fish are dying, and no one says a word."

"Now it's time for me to rant," I said to Dave. "Getting people involved in conservation groups like our local Trout Unlimited Chapter is like trying to pull teeth from the mouth of a shark. The very fact there is any water in the river these days is thanks to our chapter's efforts. The fact there are public access points on the Ruby is thanks to our efforts too. One would think that it should not be so difficult to get folks excited about one of the best systems of trout in the world. But instead of putting aside agendas to fight for the common goal of trout preservation, all I ever get about Trout Unlimited are complaints that seem to be convenient excuses for not getting involved. New folks move here, bury their heads and lock up their property. Outfitters complain vehemently about being misunderstood, but put very little back into the resource. Fish and Game manages the resource for the lowest common denominator while locals complain that fishing 'ain't what it used to be'. New-age trout bums believe the wheels of change in backwater Montana move much too slowly for them to waste their worthy efforts. On and on it goes. I can only imagine that there were the same type of excuses responsible for the decline of salmon and steelhead on the West Coast."

"Phew," Dave said, "you better come up for air."

"I don't want to make it seem that no one cares. There are some exemplary outfitters along with ranchers and citizens who get involved. But these issues should concern everyone. At least we try to do our part here," I added, referring to the meetings attended, letters written, phone calls made and all the rods we have donated for the sake of the rivers.

"The crowding problem has really gotten a lot of attention lately," Jeff picks up on a previous thought, "but it is more a matter of learning to be courteous than anything else. Unfortunately, we never talk about that. There are six billion of us on the planet. Life is just going to get more and more crowded. We better learn to deal with it."

"And what about the landowners trying to keep us out of the rivers at the bridges with the backing of out-of-state interests who are leading the charge to overturn our stream access laws!" Wayne piped in loudly.

"If sportsmen snooze too long," Glenn concludes, "there will be very little to fight for in twenty years."

"You guys are an uplifting lot," Dave jabs, "but it all makes good sense. I have to go to Butte."

After Dave had closed the door I remarked, "I don't know if I ever want to retire."

Glenn chuckled, "We have already lived our retirement." He was referring, of course, to the flexible schedule that has allowed us all to do some really neat things over the years.

Glenn then told of a couple friends who recently retired and each died shortly afterward. "You know what that means?" He then answered his own question before anyone else could, "Don't retire! We might as well keep doing what we're doing till we can't do it anymore. It has served us well so far."

There was no argument here.

Several hours into the gluing session, we changed over to the five-strippers. Although I didn't tell Wayne, he could tell right away because they sound different rolling through the tube. Sometime during the third section I heard a *clunk* and then a curse. The belt broke that rotates the blank. It is not actually a belt, but a nylon string. Although this is not an uncommon occurrence, Wayne was quick to blame the five-sider for the problem. But before the thought of the "devil's rod" got too much into his head, I went over and drew a cross on the wall in front of him to make him feel more comfortable.

"That should help," I said, as Wayne re-strung the drive wheel with a fresh length of nylon.

"Can't hurt, I suppose" Wayne smiled while gazing upon the roughly scrawled symbol directly in front of his eyes.

"Have you finished *Zen and the Art of Motorcycle Maintenance* yet," Jeff asked me. He had just recently reread the entire book, and since Jeff loves motorcycles, I am sure he related to the discourse on an entirely different plane than I.

"Just about," I replied, "but it does take some effort. I got to a certain point years ago, and never did finish it."

"It is an intensive read," Jeff agreed. "I can't imagine putting in the kind of thought that Pirsig did to figure out what life means. And so what if you do find out? What's it get you anyway?"

"Exactly," I said in a half kidding tone. "I thought I had it all figured out once in college — during the days of burnout with both my chemistry and philosophy courses. It came to me, well, in kind of a vision."

"A lot of people saw things back then," Wayne laughed, "it was called wacky tobbaccy vision."

"No drugs for me at the time," I asserted with a grin, "chemistry was tough enough with a clear mind. In fact, I was preparing for an organic chem test on very little sleep. Taking a walk in the rain on the morning of the exam, I was just trying to clear my brain when I remember becoming transfixed with a puddle vibrating from all the raindrops. After staring at it for a while I started to conceptualize molecules of water right on down to its protons, neutrons, and electrons. Then it happened. In a flash, everything in the universe made sense. Or at least I thought it did."

"What then?" Jeff asked.

"Well, I realized that if a person really did completely understand the meaning of everything, no one else would give a crap anyway. In fact, I concluded that this person would probably be the loneliest guy in the world. But even if he tried to share the knowledge, it would probably get him crucified, especially by the modern equivalent of those who think the earth is still flat. So I snapped myself out of it, even though there are still little bits and pieces of the experience still hanging around my life — namely, an uncommon number of inexplicable coincidences and other odd occurrences. You know, similar to those stories about someone getting struck by lightning and then having strange powers because of it."

"Maybe you did get hit by lightning!" Glenn chimed in.

"Come to think of it," I thought a bit, "there was some thunder rumbling around that morning."

"Hope John Ashcroft doesn't have our shop bugged," Wayne quipped, "with this kind of talk, we'll all be breaking rocks in Cuba."

"We are pretty safe here," Glenn mused, "I can't imagine those guys having any ability to know what we are talking about."

I then continued about Pirsig's work. "There was one paragraph toward the end of the book where Pirsig implied that the inner peace a fisherman attains with a rod and a worm staring out into the water is almost identical to, if not exactly the same as, the state sought after by Hindu mystics." I stopped, considered, and then continued, "There was one small reference in the entire book about fishing, and it was profound. I was amazed that at that point Pirsig didn't just get a fly rod, ride his motorcycle down to the river, start casting away — story over."

"Good point." Jeff chortled.

"If anyone is trying to change his outlook on life, though," I deliberated, " reading his book is a must!"

I reflect a few minutes while gluing the last strip before starting preparations for cleanup. Pirsig's entire quest centered upon finding that realm he called Quality where art and science, creativity and technology, fuse together in a state of inner peace and illumination. His ongoing frustration with fulfillment of this goal seemed to reflect the universal angst that plagues all of mankind. In order to truly understand what lies beyond the shadows of our limited consciousness I believe that the human race needs a sixth sense and, at least, a fourth dimension to get the job done. But even if we could discover the truth behind all the answers of the universe, our minds do not have the capabilities to handle it anyway. So, I conclude that the solution must be the journey itself — the going, not the getting there. For me the journey is fly fishing. It is as good as any.

In my way of thinking, the secret of life is to follow a path that allows for the occasional peek of a greater reality, even if the glimpse is like looking through a glass darkly. As far as I am concerned, this is *the* cosmic carrot humanity needs to keep going, just like a trout stream that continually draws the angler to the hole just around the next bend. For me Pirsig's Quality is the same realm where fly fishing and bamboo rods, water and nature, life and death are suspended in an equilibrium that makes some sort of indefinable sense. All I know for sure is that this state provides a wonderful source of peace and harmony. Understanding why isn't the answer, but trying to understand is. And the more I understand, the less I know I think I know. But that's what the whole trip is all about!

As we conclude the gluing for the day, forty bound blanks hang in the drying closet to be assembled into fine rods sometime in the future. Cleanup consists of washing and scrubbing excess glue from everything that it has touched. I pour the leftover glue from the holding container onto a worn spot upon the floor. While everything gets put away, we all pop open cans of beer and make another "boo boy" toast to a day well spent. Our chit-chat and easy going dialog continues through another beer until Wayne gets up to head back to his shop.

"I've got work to do," he volunteers, "see ya all soon."

Then Jeff prepares to leave too. "Remember the words of Hippocrates," he proclaims while heading out the door, "Life is so short, the craft so long to learn."

"Life *is* short," I replied emphatically, "so we all better make the most of it while we can. At the rate it is flying by, I'll never have time to learn the craft."

Soon after Jeff's departure, Glenn got a call from one of his kids to join the family for some event at school.

"Time to head for the barn," Glenn sighs after a tedious week. "See you Monday."

I retire to my bench and wiggle one of the five-strip prototypes standing there. I can't wait to build a few new ones, but it will be at least another month before some blanks are ready. The little four-weight in my hand will be perfect for the *baetis* hatch on the Ruby in April. In December, it is comforting to dream about spring while quietly longing for the day that I will once again cast a wisp of bamboo in the wind of hope.

In front of me there is a spot on the wall where I plan to hang a picture of my father. It was taken a few years back, and he is proudly holding the biggest smallmouth bass of his life.

After my brother took the photo, Dad released it.

That was the last fish he ever caught.

Part II

Stand and watch, feel the rhythm. Think of the fish, the smell of the first trout of the day. Think of catching a fat brook trout. Vermicular markings invisible from above. Flanks of red, orange, blue and silver. The color combination seems to defy nature's purpose of camouflage. Think of catching a ray of sunlight, a piece of history.

This is a fish that makes using a bamboo rod, if not a necessity, an obligation.

Sex, Insects, and the Beginning of Another Season
M.C. Kanouse

Martin

A pawnshop is a peculiar wormhole of existence. Although there is a strange allure that summons a bold treasure seeker to its door, any initial charm is usually dispelled by the hardnose reality of cigarette smoke, shifty eyes, and possible shady deals. But one can't dismiss a pawnshop's fitful purpose either. This vapid haven is often the one last ray of hope for those teetering precipitously on the edge of financial desperation — though my purpose for being there that afternoon had nothing to do with dire destitution. I was acting purely upon a hot tip from a friend. Earlier in the day a guitar caught his eye through the bar-covered window, and I had returned to confirm his suspicions. Peering through the smudged plate glass painted with a list of one-word inducements: stereos, coins, jewelry, and — in big bold letters — **GUNS**, I could barely make it out among the variety of other electric and acoustic guitars. But indeed, it was a Martin!

A Wisp in the Wind

For the record, a Martin is to guitars what a Mercedes is to automobiles and what a Winston bamboo is to fly rods, respective paradigms appreciated especially by those who believe that quality in a particular field of interest is an important form of expression. Although it was unlikely that my talent would ever be a worthy match, I was convinced of one thing: such a fine instrument would have the power to make a significant statement in a life searching for purpose. And there it was — hanging on the pawnshop wall — possessing, I hoped, the magic of Excalibur. I had been plunking the strings of an old Gibson for several years. This was a great guitar too, but it wasn't a Martin! More importantly, its design didn't suit my purpose. But the Model D-18 staring down from its perch in the dingy little shop of hocked existences and broken lives was undoubtedly beckoning for my attention.

I subsequently visited the storefront nestled on a seedy Salt Lake City back street several more times. Naïve enough to stick out like a Hell's Angel at a church picnic, I was afraid to ask permission to strum a few chords. I knew, though, that if I did, the temptation to buy it would be far too difficult to resist. But part of me was also afraid that one day the guitar would be gone. Although the asking price was extremely reasonable for a six-string of that quality, I was a first year teacher in a Catholic high school. There was little money to spare.

To say that the late sixties was a difficult time for our nation doesn't even begin to address how close the country came to total meltdown in an era when every standard upon which our social structure balanced was dissected, questioned, and criticized. The scars still run deep. From jungles to campuses, there were those who sacrificed their lives in this struggle of convictions, but somehow many of us survived the firestorm. The issues were complex, but in the final analysis, the Phoenix that arose delivered a more tolerant society. For me music was the only substance I needed to survive the jigsaw of emotions, feelings, and fears that threatened to consume us all back then. When I closed my eyes and played, my spirit soared — up and away from the nebulous void that defined those days of young adulthood. Although music was one thing, having the right instrument to convey one's soul was another. I would never know its story, but when I finally cradled the Martin for the first time, the sweetness of its sound touched my troubled heart.

The very next day I borrowed enough bucks to cover a down payment. Afterwards, the friend who discovered the Martin in the first place made an offer. He volunteered to take the Gibson off my hands — for a substantial discount, of course — but I was desperate. After arranging to sell a childhood collection of buffalo nickels a few days later, I had gathered almost enough to close the sale by the end of the week. Money in hand, it was off to the pawnshop.

The pawnbroker was an elderly, stubble-faced gent with short white hair, and he was astute enough to assess my young and obvious poor comportment right from the beginning. Fortunately, he wasn't the sort to drive a hard bargain. From a dusty, dimly lit corner of discarded valuables and lung-choking smoke, the shrewd veteran of pawn cast a scornful eye through his wire rims. We haggled a bit, but the caretaker of shattered dreams finally assessed that there was no more blood in this turnip. He eventually settled for what I had by announcing from the gloom of his yellowed world, "Son, you got yourself one hell of a deal!" Within a few minutes, Martin and I headed home. It was September 1969. For several years afterwards, we played beautiful music together.

Reflecting the sentiments of Isaac Walton, Roderick Haig-Brown once wrote that angling "is the contemplative man's recreation, and contemplative men are naturally inclined to recollect emotion in tranquility." He concluded that many of these emotions are evident in the volumes of angling literature handed down throughout the years. One may further speculate whether these same emotions have inspired the modern-era proliferation of artists and craftsmen as well, particularly in the field of fly fishing. In addition to writing, emotional expression has also become manifest in a variety of other creative permutations from fly-tying to wood carving to watercolors. The rekindled interest in building bamboo rods is surely an outgrowth of the same process. For the philosophical angler, this entire movement raises a question. Do angling and its environs enkindle this contemplative expression, or are all these contemplative artisans merely attracted to angling? Although seeking an answer could enkindle much thought-provoking discussion, for me I'd have to say it was a little of both. With the help of the Martin, it was music that eventually led back to my childhood love — fishing.

By 1972, the war was over. Many years of deep thought and turmoil spawned a soul of restlessness. Although a career of blind commitment is a noble goal for some, I wanted to explore roads less conventional. So I quit teaching, traveled around the country, and sang about beautiful places and lost loves. Along the way, the works of Joe Brooks taught me about the ways of trout. But my meandering did not survive the scrutiny of many respected relatives and advisors. In their minds my aspirations were aimlessly adrift, most certainly lacking the sufficient direction to satisfy the traditional expectations many had placed on my life. In those days, following the wishes of others was a matter of protocol. Consequently, I enrolled in graduate school. Apparently, music and trout weren't enough for those interested in my long-term welfare.

But after what my generation went through, nothing else made sense.

A vision is a difficult phenomenon to explain — metaphysically, philosophically, religiously, or any other "kind-of-ly." But if I had to take a stab, I would call it an indescribable event of the spirit that causes an epiphany in one's life. According to those astute enough to know about such matters, a vision can take place in various ways, shapes, or forms. And if such an unexplainable event should ever occur, it is best just to accept it. So I am not going to speculate, but one morning in early 1974 something happened in the form of a dream — a dream I could never remember. Of one thing I was certain. Upon awakening, my destiny couldn't have been more defined even if AAA had sent a package of maps pointing out the direction. The message was clear: *Go forth, young man, and fish.*

Naturally, quitting graduate school the next day was deemed in order. Who was I to argue? Though one could debate, I suppose, that this dream-event seemed conveniently self-serving, the call for me to do it far outweighed everyone's suspicions. Once the decision was made, then the proper arrangements for the impending mission needed to be addressed. First of all, the fact that I had no money was a serious consideration. But since I had only one valuable possession to my name, I really had no choice. So, maybe it was just to prove the purity of my intentions, or, possibly to demonstrate the power of the purported dream, but when I sold my prized guitar to an acquaintance in order to finance this spectral "call to fish," I was committed.

No one said that following a vision would be easy, and deep sadness emphasized the point on that day the Martin left my possession. Afterwards, it still took another month to tie up the loose ends of an alleged "aimless" existence.

But once June arrived, I loaded everything, including an old traveling guitar, into a Datsun pickup and headed toward Montana. One chapter ends. A new chapter begins. As Salt Lake disappeared in a cloud of exhaust, I never looked back.

The road led to adventure and it led to hardship. It led to jobs and eventually, marriage. But importantly, it led to trout. First, it was the Dolly Varden (Note: now bull trout) of Northern Idaho, then the westslope cutthroat of central Idaho's wilderness called. After a few years the Big Hole browns lured me back to Montana. More and more, trout became the song I sang, and the fly rod was the instrument. I played the music wherever there was a river, but I never forgot the old Martin that made it all possible. In fact, for many years I was able to track the whereabouts of the D-18. But like a beautiful sunset, it eventually disappeared into the obscurity of passing time as old friends faded into fond memory. Although I never doubted the decision, I always wondered what this journey meant. And since lessons are learned along the way of any quest, one never knows when or where they are learned. I am told it's a Zen thing. In time, certain truths become apparent.

It has been over twenty years since I first stumbled into the rod shop in Twin Bridges. Being in the right spot at the right time led to a job a few months later. For over seventy-five years the Winston Rod Company has been serving the fly fishing industry. In an age where the contemplative gives way to the competitive, this fact may not seem as significant as it really should. But since we are all products of what has gone before us, and since this company has spanned decades of the modern era of fly fishing, it would be foolhardy for the serious fly angler to dismiss these facts as unimportant. Throughout a good

portion of the American fly fishing scene, the Winston
Rod Company has been there — and my fishing journey
had led me to its front door.

For those who do not know, Glenn Brackett is a former
owner of Winston. But after his interests were sold in the
early nineties, he still continued on in the company as
one of the world's foremost bamboo rod makers. In fact,
some folks reverently refer to him as "the bamboo guru"
— a label that he would much rather decline to
acknowledge. To those who are able to judge such matters,
his career confirms that contemplative tranquility is still
a valued aspect of fly fishing. Jeff and I have worked closely
with him over the years. To the both of us, he is a
charismatic leader who believes that solitude, fly fishing,
meditation and working with one's hands all converge in
the bamboo shop, creating a spiritual refuge for weary
anglers battered by the mercenary overtones of the nineties
approach to trout. Glenn is not a bottom-line kind of guy.
In his mind, the world of trout and the crafting of bamboo
rods should be the means to a greater good, and if they
don't make one a better person, then what's the point!

When Glenn was eight years old, his grandfather would
take him to visit the old Winston shop in downtown San
Francisco. It was after meeting Lew Stoner, one of the
original owners working diligently at his trade, that Glenn
determined his calling in life was to build bamboo rods
for Winston. The company has had just a handful of owners
over its illustrious history, and until the late eighties, only
a handful of employees. After Doug Merrick bought the
company from Stoner, he employed Gary Howells, who
eventually became a well-known artisan in his own realm.
Glenn learned the craft from Gary and then became co-
owner of the company with Tom Morgan in the seventies.
Since then he has trained Jeff Walker. In subsequent years,
it has been my privilege to help them both out. Glenn has

known almost everyone ever associated with the company, and he has been a loyal friend to them all. In fact, he visited both Doug and Gary regularly until their deaths. Through Glenn's meticulous attention to details, it has been his passion to absorb every ounce of knowledge and spirit he has gleaned from the past and incorporate all he has gathered into each bamboo rod we build today.

In the local community Glenn selflessly works with disadvantaged youth. Also, because he believes the world would perish if it could no longer sustain wild trout, he actively supports all resource issues around the country. A voice of encouragement to his friends, there is not one of us who hasn't cried on his shoulder a time or two either. His advice usually comes in the form of one-liners inspired by a Zen connection to a Greater Source. "Do the right things for the right reason" or "stay true to the inner self and good things will happen," echoes the gentle regard he has for everyone and everything. Since he believes each life follows the path of a fleeting butterfly, he also believes that there are always lessons to be learned along the way to keep us pointed in the right direction. Enlightenment can come from the most insignificant events as well as from the big ones.

One story stands out to illustrate the spirit of our bamboo world. It happened during a cold February several years ago when a self-proclaimed mountain man was hitchhiking his way through town to a warmer place of survival. From his animal skin hat, shoulder-length hair and long-straggled beard to his caribou-lined mukluks, the fellow fit the part perfectly. Everything he needed to survive *anywhere* was in his pack; and, as it turned out, this was everything he owned. When two guys in a Ford pickup finally pulled over, the man from the mountains tossed his backpack into the cargo bed. But just as he was getting into the cab, the truck sped off. In sub-zero temperatures two ignorant yahoos left the wayfarer standing on a corner in Twin Bridges — without one possession.

Within a few hours, Glenn found him, dazed and disoriented, wandering the frozen sidewalks of our small town. Without hesitation he set up a cot in the bamboo shop and immediately organized a community effort to help the forlorn fellow get his life back together. His name was Tony. For several weeks Glenn, Jeff and I befriended the colorful stranger whose character was accentuated by thick glasses that would regularly slip down his nose. His story was a sad one. Leaving an abusive family situation in Texas when he was fifteen, he had been on the road ever since. By the time of this predicament, he was in his late thirties. Although there were many gaps in his life story, he claimed to have spent recent years camping in the mountains throughout the West, getting by on ingenuity and determination. Whether or not any of his tales were true didn't faze Glenn. Tony was definitely lost, in need of help, and it was the role of the bamboo shop to do something about it. "If fly fishing doesn't inspire us to do what's right," he would reflect, "then we'd better just turn off the lights."

Tony got a kick out of the entire bamboo process. "Let me get this straight," he once concluded, habitually using two fingers to push his heavy glasses up and onto the bridge his nose, "you build bamboo fishin' poles, sell em for tousands of dollars so people can catch fish just to release em." He laughed, " Geeze. That's really sumptin'!" By the end of his stay, Tony still understood very little about our world, but he was overwhelmed with appreciation for what the town had done for him. Folks from around the area had replaced his equipment, raised some traveling money, and bought him a bus ticket to any destination of his choice. A few days before his departure, the two jerks who stranded him were apprehended, but only a few of Tony's personal items were recovered. When I dropped him off at the bus station, he could not contain his grateful tears. A few years later, Tony contacted Glenn. He was managing a McDonald's somewhere in Colorado.

In the bamboo shop I have learned that the process encompasses much more than the making of bamboo fly rods. Indeed, lessons have come in many forms. Often, they are much subtler than the episode with Tony, but with every new experience there is a story that, in turn, gives birth to insight. Although my guitar-playing days were behind me, the rhythms of flowing waters have replaced the songs that I once sang from the depths of my heart. Too quickly the years have passed since Salt Lake City, but I still fish as much now, maybe even more. The journey has led to a better place, and fly fishing has certainly taken on a new perspective. But if there was ever any doubt about following that dream in the seventies, a phone call put it to rest in the late nineties.

When I answered, his voice was pleasantly familiar. Danny was a freshman when I began to teach in 1969. He was consumed by music during his high school years, and after earning a college degree, he eventually made a successful musical career for himself by playing the nightclub circuit. We maintained minimum contact after I hit the road, but it was always good to hear from him when he phoned. After catching up on all the important matters of mutual interest, he popped an intriguing question that likely prompted his call.

"Guess what?"

After my obvious response of acknowledgement, he continued casually. "I found your Martin hanging on the wall of an old pawnshop."

I fell silent. It had been twenty-odd years, and for most of them the guitar had vanished into the sea of penniless musicians. I figured it would have gotten lost, or more likely destroyed, in the shuffle of human activity somewhere during that period. Anyway, I had put the memory of the D-18 behind me long ago.

"It can't be," were the words of skepticism I redirected to Danny. "How do you know it's *my* guitar?"

Danny loved the Martin too, and he often played it in the old days when he had the chance. "Don't you remember?" His question pleaded. "You wrote your name in the bridging underneath the sound hole. On a hunch I peeped in, and there it was!"

I was still struggling with a flash of emotions when Dan continued. "The pawnbroker's asking four times what you originally paid for it. But I could probably get him down. Do you want it?" Sensing my hesitation, he then added, "If not, I'll buy it anyway."

Since there was already another guitar sitting in my closet gathering dust, I really didn't need one more parked next to it doing the same thing. But I told Danny I'd get back to him in a day or two.

Later, when I recounted the phone conversation to my wife, Debra was moved by the story. "It has come full circle," was her initial comment. Although the Martin was before her time, she insisted that I buy it. "For whatever reason, it seems like you were meant to have it," was her sage conclusion. "You wouldn't be where you are now if it wasn't for that guitar. After all, it financed your lifelong fishing trip."

So the next day I made formal arrangements with Danny. He played the D-18 in his band until the following summer when he personally delivered the classic instrument during a visit to Montana. After a long journey of its own, the Martin had finally returned home.

Not too long afterward, I fielded another call. The fellow on the other end wanted to find out about a used Winston bamboo rod he had discovered browsing the second hand shops of Spokane. The old bamboo triggered a significant memory from his past; so he decided to investigate it further. Since we always like to hear about old rods, I encouraged him to continue. Whether they have been lost, broken, or handed down throughout the generations, these types of stories are always touching in one way or the other.

"Years ago, I'd say, October of '72," the caller started, "I was hunting chukars near the Grande Ronde River, close to where I live in Washington State. My dogs and I were headed back to the truck when we happened upon a fly fisherman. As we approached, he was just landing a beautiful steelhead on a brand new bamboo that he had recently received as a retirement gift. He was so proud of the rod that he told me all about it. From that day on, I always remembered that it was a Winston. As it turned out, this was the second steelhead he had landed that morning. The Grande Ronde was a good river back then. But since the fellow was a former high school superintendent in Spokane, he never got the chance to fish in the fall. So these were the first two steelhead he had ever caught."

The man continued to reminisce, "I recall that morning like it was yesterday: the steelhead, the rod, and the beauty of the entire scene. I didn't fly fish back then, but I was so affected by the experience that I started shortly afterwards."

It seems that the rod this caller had just discovered in the shop was built for steelhead fishing, but it was hardly ever used. Taken in on trade several months beforehand, it was the understanding of the shopkeeper that this particular cane rod had only caught two steelhead in its history.

"Do your records indicate who would have originally owned rod #1143?" He asked. "I vaguely remember the name of the angler on 'the Ronde' that day, but I'm sure I'd recognize it if I heard it again."

Often our records do document original owners and where they lived. When I checked, there was a name. Rod #1143 was completed in 1972 for a fellow who lived in Spokane. Indeed, the rod in the shop once belonged to the retired superintendent whom the caller had chanced upon so long ago.

"Wow!" was the response. The astonished caller then asked, " If you were me, would you buy it?"

I then narrated a brief version of my Martin's homecoming. "For whatever reason," I concluded by using my wife's exact words, "it seems like you were meant to have it."

He agreed.

"Your rods are magical," the fellow said before hanging up.

There *is* something special about the rods we build. It is undeniable. You can feel the spirit in our shop. You can sense the magic in the completed work. This spring Glenn went to China in an effort to trace raw bamboo back to its source. For him, this was the last piece in *his* lifetime journey that would bring all the intangible elements together in the ultimate expression of fly fishing art — a Winston bamboo fly rod. A circle! The beginning becomes the end, and the end becomes the beginning. The meaning is lost with any attempt to think about it too much.

Before he departed for the Far East, Glenn wanted to show me a letter. At that point he was well aware of the Martin and the role it played it my career. "Thought you'd like to see this one," was all Glenn said as he handed me the envelope.

Like so many other notes we receive, the sentences praised the beauty and impeccable craftsmanship of the rod that the proud new owner had just received. For me, however, there was meaning that extended far beyond the message as the words reached back to that pawnshop in 1969. In my mind the circle that started way back then was now complete as well. For the letter Glenn wanted me to read in a quiet corner of the shop was signed by the CEO of *Martin & Co.* — maker of fine guitars.

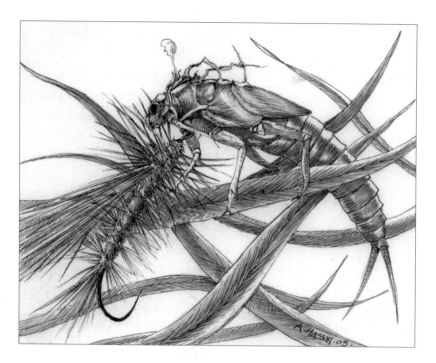

Fifty-Fifty

There's nothing more uplifting than an outing on the river, especially when all routine affairs have been put to rest beforehand and the only care in the world, at least for the day, is your choice of a fly. Such was the case when, with great expectations, I approached the Bitterroot River on what promised to be a splendid morning for late March. According to the angling grapevine, *the* hatch was on — though it is highly questionable what that assessment actually means. The *skwala* is a medium-sized, dark green colored stonefly which has stirred quite an early season fervor of interest around the land amongst those who fly fish, particularly throughout the nineties. This unique phenomenon occurs in fishable numbers on some rivers of Western Montana from mid March through early April. The size eight *skwala*, as it is commonly acknowledged, emerges on the quiet edges of slow moving water and then drifts for great distances upon the surface, often sitting still as a stick. The fish love them. Even when there are only a few around, once the trout have developed their early season appetite for these mouthful morsels, attractor patterns will bring many fish to the surface for those anglers willing to pound the water with a stimulator or other favorite imitations.

On this particularly fine day I had worked my way up the river a good mile from a public access point below Hamilton. The thin layer of clouds flattened the existing sunlight while muted shadows breathed a warmth more associated with mid April. As late morning ushered an increase in air temperature, the first skwala floated by — and without fail, a hungry trout intercepted it along the way. It should be noted that the fish in the Bitterroot aren't dumb; so even a well placed imitation doesn't always produce a rise. But on this morning several trout were willing to give serious consideration to what I had to offer. All was good! That is, until a sudden realization hit me. At that exact moment of cranial registration, the same flash hit the pit of my stomach like a bad baloney sandwich.

I am a law abiding citizen, and that has always been the case. I am sure this has as much to do with nurturing as anything else. In my family there has never been any option other than doing the right thing. Another explanation, I suppose, was my religion. As a former Catholic I was born with a propensity for guilt. This compulsive leaning may be due to a genetic predilection coming from a long line of believers molded in that persuasion. It is hard to describe guilt. More like an eternal nagging than an emotion, the beauty of guilt lies in the fact that it makes folks very uncomfortable — so unpleasant, in fact, that it forces them to be good even if they don't want to be. Thanks to this affliction, looking over my shoulder even when there is no apparent reason has always been a part of my make up. It's like waiting for a great eternal shoe to drop in judgment of something you are sure you did, but you don't know what. This Kafkaesque cloud of uncertainty keeps many religions in business. The inner gnawing, like a mouse in the wall, lies just below the surface in wait of something to be truly concerned about.

In Montana everybody's fishing license expires on February 28th, unless, of course, it is leap year. I even made the effort in 1992 to catch a few fish in the Yellowstone River on the 29th of February just for the novelty of it. The added pleasure of squeezing the last extra drop out of this official document was especially satisfying. Normally, being compelled to do the right thing leads me straight to the local convenience store on the morning of March 1st to purchase the permit for another year. But it was pushing late March that day on the Bitterroot, and I had already been fishing several times during the month. So when the awareness struck in an instant of mindless lucidity that the ritual to renew my fishing license for the present season was irresponsibly neglected earlier in the month, pleasure turned into pure panic. Then, instant paranoia. At that moment I was sure that the aforementioned cosmic shoe would drop in the form of a lightning bolt. Immediately, I was convinced that somehow the local warden had already figured out my scheme. That inner gnawing had me mired in the belief that the trap had already been set to bring me to justice, to mete out retribution commensurate to the scum-sucking lowlife I had instantaneously become. For sure, the verdict would read: BANISHED FROM ALL RIVERS FOR LIFE. And guilt, in the religious sense, does not discriminate between innocent civil slip-ups or blatant moral blunders. It is bad enough to fish part of a day without a license, that may even be excusable, but to get away with it for a whole month catapulted me into the realm of shamelessness that even a few thousand Hail Marys couldn't rectify. Staying out of jail was one thing, staying out of hell was altogether another.

On top of it my dread of game wardens is not without foundation. It dates back to a story I once read by Patrick McManus many years ago. Where he grew up in Northern Idaho lived the legendary warden, Darcy Sneed. It seemed Sneed had this built-in radar which was able to detect any violator perpetrating any type of wildlife crime in his jurisdiction at any time, day or night. As a youth, McManus indicated he couldn't get away with anything without Sneed knowing about it. The guy had an uncanny omnipresence which prompted many to theorize there were actually several Sneeds based upon multiple, simultaneous sightings on any given day. This is the kind of story a person with a guilt tempered background shouldn't be reading.

My fear was further fortified by first hand horror stories of folks throughout the West who knew of some poor citizen getting nabbed for a violation of inadvertent negligence. In fact, you'd never even hear of anyone who was caught actually doing something really bad like possessing too many deer or lugging away a cooler full of fish, but tales about the sorry soul who forgot to pinch the barb on his fly or something similarly innocuous were rampant. To add to the anxiety, at one point in my career I had been checked on the stream at least twenty times in several states. In fact, once on White Sand Creek in central Idaho, two conservation officers crashed through the bush like a couple of grizzlies in a bacon factory to surround me while I was casting flies to small cutthroats. With guns drawn they came at me from two directions, and after asking a few questions, they left me there to "enjoy" the rest of the day. In all other instances, I came up clean too, but for years afterwards I had a permanent crimp in my neck from always checking my backside.

The first reaction to my reversal of fortune on the Bitterroot that day was to jump into the high grass and lie prone until dark. But damn, the fishing was too good to blow off the rest of the afternoon. Although continuing on wasn't even a consideration, I figured a low profile route back to the parking area would be the only wise alternative. So with visions of Sneed dancing through my head, I took a dewatered side channel that led to a little bigger channel. Wading knee deep downstream, the use of some rip rap along the bank completely blocked this clandestine withdrawal from general view. For the final five hundred yards I ducked behind cottonwoods and crawled through willows until, at last, I was sitting in the front seat of my rig. Although I didn't notice until later that the tip of my favorite bamboo rod broke in the process of my stealthy retreat, I just wrote it off as a form of penance for my unforgivable *faux pas*. But before heading down to the convenience store to buy a license, I dug into my lunch. Sure enough, though it shouldn't have been much of a surprise, the local warden drove through the parking area shortly after my first bite. As his rig circled the fishing access site and then rolled on by, I slid down in my seat with a mouthful of sandwich tucked firmly against my uvula.

After this narrow escape my senses were in high alert; my guilt sensors never worked better. A few weeks later I took an accomplished young angler over to explore Rock Creek. Eric had just moved to Twin Bridges from St. Louis to learn how to build bamboo rods, and he never before had the opportunity to catch a westslope cutthroat. The cool and cloudy afternoon was shaping up nicely for a possible western march brown hatch, but Eric's first ever cutthroat came attached to a woolly bugger. Although it was only for a brief period, we were treated to a spurt of size #14 duns late in the day. As hoped, these hefty mayflies attracted the attention of some nice westslopes. When the hatch suddenly came to a halt we headed back toward Philipsburg, but not without making one last stop. The evening chill bordered on uncomfortable, and the patches of snow along this portion of the creek further intensified the bite in the air. Eric headed upstream, and I took up position two holes below.

Making a deliberate pass through a favorite stretch of mine which spanned over twenty-five years, I started in the tailout, working the run with upstream casts. In the process, only one nice fish made a serious boil below my dry fly offering. There was a day when I would have made the appropriate fly change to deal with the situation, but just knowing that fish was in the same place where there always has been one was pleasure enough. Continuing on, I methodically worked up to the head of the pool. The series of "last casts" had begun when something caught my eye in the darkening water of late evening. Peering into the slack break off the main riffle, I saw a dead fish sitting on the bottom. Usually such discoveries are either a whitefish or a sucker wantonly killed and discarded by a misguided angler. But the white edges of the exposed fins as well as the size of the carcass indicated this to be an intriguing find. With one kick of my boot, the fish flipped off the gravel and suspended long enough for a quick, cold grab. Fish now in hand, I checked thoroughly, and it was just as I had suspected. The rather beefy creature was a twenty inch bull trout, its coloration was sharp and its details were still intact. Remembering a few tangles with bull trout over the years, undoubtedly this particular fish would have been fine quarry at the end of one's leader.

Upon further inspection, it appeared that this beauty had just recently perished, and the reason was conspicuously apparent. Three staples in its abdomen closed a two inch gash which likely concealed a radio transmitter, the antenna of which stuck three inches or more out the poor critter's anal orifice. The bull trout, a native predator to the waters of the northern Rockies west of the divide, belongs to the branch of salmonids known as the chars. The lake trout, brook trout and Dolly Varden are its cousins. With its declining populations, this particular fish was probably a part of a telemetry study designed to accumulate data which optimistically would lead to the survival of this native species in the future. Unfortunately, this fish died in the name of science, and one can only hope it wasn't in vain. I took the bull trout over to the shoreline, and laid it on a big chunk of snow.

Realizing Eric had probably never seen a bull trout either, I figured the dead fish would make for an ideal on-site clinic. Upon retrieving my young fishing companion, we then poked, prodded and discussed the subject matter — its prognosis and its plight. After the biology class concluded, the question subsequently arose concerning the disposal of the fish with the enclosed apparatus still in place. Knowing full well that the value of such a device warranted special consideration, we tried to figure out a course of action. When I boldly suggested taking the fish to the nearest game warden, Eric looked at me like I was nuts. "What if you get fined for having an out-of-season fish in your possession," he asked.

Blinded once again by trying to do the right thing, panic set in — immediately! Speaking with wisdom beyond his years, there was no doubt that Eric's words made great sense. What the hell was I thinking, especially after the close escape a few weeks ago on the Bitterroot. Then a twisted sense of guilt once again set in for even thinking of something so depraved, visions of a mythical Sneed stepping out of the woods right then-and-there were prompted by the irrational paranoia welling up inside me. I respectfully took the remains of the bull trout and placed it in the shallow edges of Rock Creek, but only after I had carefully wiped it down for fingerprints. This time, however, no warden lurked anywhere along the entire stretch back home.

The next day I made an anonymous phone call to the Fish, Wildlife and Parks office in Deer Lodge — the home of the state penitentiary, I might add. Talking to a senior biologist, I told him of my dilemma after detailing the exact whereabouts of the dead bull trout with the transmitter. I suggested that turning on the receiver would be the best way to locate its exact position. No comment ensued.

"If you were me," I asked with some trepidation, "what would you have done?"

Without hesitation the biologist replied," I would have tried to do the right thing by taking it to a local warden." "But," he then added after a brief, reflective pause, "it would probably be fifty-fifty."

"Fifty-Fifty?" I asked with a tone of cautious curiosity.

"You never know about wardens," he stated in a serious voice. "Some would have probably given you a ticket." As if I could hear him thoughtfully scratching his chin through the phone line, he concluded, " Yup, I'd say, about a fifty-fifty chance."

"And what would that have cost me?"

"Oh boy," the state employee exclaimed as he drew in a deep breath, "probably a few thousand dollars. You have to realize, the bull trout is a threatened species."

A long silence prevailed. Because I am a great believer in game laws as well as the Endangered Species Act, I didn't want to sound impertinent. Since the bull trout had just recently been listed as threatened in Montana, all the ramifications of this official designation had not yet registered. The way I see it, my fines could have ended up covering the cost of the entire scientific project. Heck! Every now and then, I figured, my religious upbringing really comes in handy. A little misguided guilt isn't so bad after all.

As for paranoia. No problem either! I hung up before the guy at the Fish, Wildlife, and Parks office could possibly trace the call.

The Eagle Talisman

Since the search for steelhead had led to exploring the intimate rivers and quiet waters of Vancouver Island, my mind wasn't prepared for the distressing news it was about to hear. In fact, only those who have established a meaningful relationship with a pet could possibly understand the anguish. The listless disposition our dog exhibited several weeks prior to my departure was just another phase of an older age. Or so we thought. But as Debra read the veterinary report over the phone in a voice amazingly composed for the information it was bearing, my heart sank into deep sadness. The well travelled Lhasa apso and world's most unlikely fishing buddy was diagnosed with aggressive lymphoma carcinoma. In another words, a very bad form of cancer. Since words couldn't express our feelings, our conversation, twisted with emotion, came to a silent conclusion. The dog was my wife's soulful companion, as well.

I finished out the rest of the afternoon fishing in a muddle of sorrow. As I drove the eight hundred miles home the next day, I recounted the years of memories Tibby provided, amidst a tearful lament of how quickly the time had passed. From the Penobscot in Maine to the Henry's Fork in Idaho to the Klamath in California, she was there, enjoying the sights while giving indifferent approval each time another fish came to be released. According to the vet, she had less than two months to live.

The night before she died, I had a dream. It was peaceful, but somber still the same. In that abstract state of slumber our terminally ill companion got out of her death bed and stood there as if all her burdens had been lifted. Excited and relieved, I yelled in thankful exuberance, "Tibby, old girl, you're better!" She turned, looked at me one last time and then walked away — fading off into a distant light. Waking in a sudden jolt of reality, the first impulse to check upon the validity of the pseudo-vision was automatic. I ran downstairs. Realizing the inevitable could occur at any time, my wife and I just didn't want her to die alone. This was the least we could do for thirteen years of faithful friendship. Being there was the last act of love we could bestow upon her. But as I quietly approached her comfortable chair, my apprehension was greeted by an attentive stare. Now thoroughly incapacitated by the disease that had relentlessly spread throughout her rotund body in only eight weeks, the decision had been made to comfort her until the pain was obvious. How we dreaded the final journey to end her suffering! Later that day, however, she licked my hand one last time, and then, while tending to her needs, her troubles dissolved forever into a restful peace. In a moment the spirit drained from her body, silent and still. Touching her head in a final act of comfort, I sobbed like a child.

In ancient folklore it was believed that after God had made all creatures He then created a chasm between the animals and humans. But just before the gulf widened, the dog leapt over to sit by the side of man. Who can deny there is a special link between the human and the canine species, particularly for those willing to cultivate that bond? Perhaps it is the mystery, the not knowing how they communicate or why they care, but when it comes to dogs and those who know them, there is an undeniable something. Between the lines there is a sense of transcendence that extends beyond the obvious.

Recent studies note the significant impact a dog can have on a human life. It is a proven fact that folks with canine companions have lower blood pressure. They even live longer lives. I have never had a hunting dog, but those of us who know bird hunters can hardly bring up the topic of bygone four-legged comrades without the mist of a distant past welling up in their eyes. Dogs know more than we could ever imagine. They tell us more than we could ever understand. I was convinced that my dream was a powerful message. It was Tibby's way of saying her last good bye. After all, I'm sure she figured, that was the least she could do for us.

It may seem strange to those who cannot relate, but dealing with her loss was no easy matter. Among the many downsides of growing older is the increased rate of passing among family members, friends, and yes, even pets. For whom the bell tolls — a prospect we all must face. Memories — good, bad, happy, sad — play an increasingly larger role in shaping the wisdom of our elder years. If for no other reason, the longer you live, the more memories you have gathered. When a friend passes, dealing with the memories is a most difficult task. For me, music helps. And though pure absorption of sound tends to muffle or maybe even sooth the ghosts rattling in the corners of an otherwise sound mind, only time dulls the immediate sting.

My first recollection of a true memory was dealing with the gut twisting departure from a high school sweetheart during my initial year of college. The wind, the moon, a summer day all somehow seemed different after we said good bye, as it turned out, forever. As a kid you just remember things. But later in life, when remembering has a host of emotions attached, memory then takes on a whole new level of meaning.

At this point in life, though, there can be just as much pleasure attached to a memory as discomfort. For instance, paging through my fishing log in front of a winter fire can stimulate wonderful thoughts that can lead to a vicarious adventure without leaving the easy chair. Even when fishing, I actually seem to get more pleasure remembering the whens, wheres, and hows of past fish than in the effort it takes to duplicate the experience in the present tense. So when it came to my dog and all the escapades we shared over the years the sadness is more than offset by the remembrance of happy times. But getting over her would not be easy, since part of me feared forgetting her entirely. Because her impact on my life was not trivial, I did not want to trivialize her death. So I dwelled on the joyful occasions we shared. Also since many folks don't understand this bond, I wrestled with the concept alone, listening to the soothing music of my favorite rivers. As the trout danced, my heart looked for solace.

In the development of our nation, it is the loss of the Native American perspective that is likely the most tragic casuality of progress. The intuitive connection to the earth and its creatures was once essential to the survival of indigenious peoples. The role of birds, fish and mammals was captured and passed on through generations of ritual and lore. This belief system emanated from the wholeness of life as natural to them as a drink of water. These days technological man looks for answers in traditional religion, new age cults, multi-step programs, motivational clinics, evangelical preachings or even astrological phone calls to deal with fragmented existences and scattered identities. But, in an ironic sort of twist, the American Indian presently tends to the remnants of a once proud heritage in forgotten corners of the country still bearing the very kernels of insight many spend so much effort searching elsewhere to find. While we scurry about in fear of what the Hard Drive Deity has in store for us in the era of Y2K and beyond, for me simple truth still reigns at the edge of a trout river. There earth, water, sky, air, wind and life come together in a tapestry of sensations — a weaving of color and sound, feelings and emotions. Somehow trout keep me focused on the ways of the Native past that have otherwise evaporated in the heat of modern existence. As odd as it may seem, somehow my dog kept me in touch with the genuine spirit of life which those who once lived so close to the earth knew so much about.

Although it seemed troublesome to be bothered so much by the death of a dog, I couldn't put it behind me for months on end. Maybe it was because Tibby was the first dog in my life that made it from puppyhood all the way to death by natural causes, or maybe it was more. Somehow I felt she was an embodiment that intuititively connected me to a spiritual plane around which I was constantly scratching the edges. Whatever it was that unsettled my emotions, I just needed to find some way to close the door.

The rain fell steadily on what would be my last day of fishing for steelhead in British Columbia for the year. Rain has a way of settling the dust which occasionally clouds the mind, a natural cleansing that opens the pores of both thought and insight. Though I never choose to fish in the rain, I rarely shy away from it either — especially when the grayness gradually builds while already on the water, culminating in precipitation that totally immerses the experience as if the river has become one with the atmosphere.

From the time my brother flew back to Buffalo the day before, the clouds had been dripping steadily for twenty-four hours straight. That morning the dampness was particularly uncomfortable, but the long walk would likely melt away the chill. As the droplets tapped a beat upon the hood of my Gortex jacket on the long hike back to a run that had produced several fish over the years, I reveled in the splendid steelhead moments spent with Rick the past ten days. Stitching together many thoughts, one at a time, I realized that getting back to the world of reality would be difficult because my dog would not be there. Fortunately, the mesmerizing pursuit of this magnificent sea-run rainbow trout provided the needed escape and brief respite to avoid dealing with the sadness.

Glenn Brackett was planning to join me later in the week, but the long-range weather prospects were bleak. Although rain typically revitalizes any steelhead river, there is a point beyond which the effort becomes hopeless. The water rises and the fish manifest a non-responsive nature until the situation turns around and conditions begin to improve. The water had already come up six inches, and there was no end in sight. It seemed that the point of no return had been reached. The water was tinged with gray. Deadness prevailed. When a steelhead river "blows out," the sensible angler normally uses the time for more constructive purposes.

At camp the previous evening I talked to Glenn on the pay phone unsheltered from the driving rain. Given the impending conditions, Glenn decided to forgo the frustrations associated with the uncertain waiting for high water to recede back into fishing shape — especially after a fifteen hundred mile trip. Although I was looking forward to spending time on the water with this humble friend and bamboo legend, I had little patience either to endure the tempest. This was a troublesome system passing through northwestern British Columbia, and the effects of early October storms have a way of lingering on for quite a while.

After putting the idea to rest, we concluded our discussion with a tone of regret. But then, just before hanging up, Glenn made a special request. Prior to returning to Montana he asked me to catch one last fish for Tom Morgan, his former partner as owner of the Winston Rod Company. Since Glenn and I both believe in the power of symbolism, entreaties of this nature are not taken lightly — especially between the two of us. Tom lies incapacitated these days, suffering from the effects of MS, but he still designs the rods his wife Gerri builds at their custom rod company called *Tom Morgan Rodsmiths*. Having worked with Tom for many years, I can testify that he is an inspiration to those of us still fortunate enough to have our health. Although he can no longer fish, he is always thrilled to hear stories about the trout and steelhead he still loves. But considering the present status of the weather, I reluctantly indicated to Glenn that fulfilling his wish for Tom may be darn near impossible. Then I reminded him of the promise he made to another friend a few years ago just before we left to fish the Bulkley for a week. I heard him smiling through the pay phone, no doubt recalling the burden he placed upon himself that entire trip.

Doug Merrick was the renowned maker of cane rods who owned Winston until Tom Morgan purchased the company in 1974. Just prior to our departure that year,

Doug had a debilitating stroke that would eventually claim his life a year later. Understanding the gravity of the situation, Glenn made a special trip to visit him at the hospital in San Francisco. Upon his return, Glenn updated the concerned folks at Winston about Doug's dire condition. Although death seemed imminent, the former bamboo master was still communicative, but barely. That was all Glenn told us.

Three of us made that particular trip to BC in 1996 — Glenn, myself and Jeff Walker, second in command of Winston's modern bamboo regime. We were accompanied, as well, by a variety of cane steelhead rods made for the occasion. Unfortunately, though, the steelhead were not too cooperative during the eight days that we fished together. In fact, there seemed to be a dearth of fish throughout the entire section of river to which we were casting our flies. There was no sign of anything for days. Eventually, a few steelhead found the Waller Wakers Jeff and I were skating, but the fish continued to elude Glenn. Other than for a few boils here and there, he remained "snake-bitten" for eight days straight. But such matters don't seem to bother Glenn much. Well aware of the unexplainable inequities that the Steelhead Gods can bestow, he has caught his fair share over the years. Personally, I am never comfortable at steelhead camp until everyone has hooked a fish. Nevertheless, Glenn was content, though he seemed to persist with a fervor uncommon to his easy-going nature.

On the very last night of that trip dusk was one notch away from total darkness as Jeff and I had already downed a few Molson's to commemorate the conclusion of the "boo boy" gathering. But at this point, there was no sign of Glenn. Normally, this would be of no concern, but Glenn was floating down the Bulkley that evening in his canoe. Making our way to the shoreline below our campsite, we began to scan the water for signs of our wayward friend. Fortunately, it didn't take long to resolve our anxiety. With much relief we could barely make out his silhouette on the opposing shore at the head of the up-river run. After a few more moments passed, we then watched as his ghostly figure hopped into his vessel. Maneuvering the well-used aluminum craft skillfully out of the blackened backdrop and through the white licks of rolling river, he gently guided it to where Jeff and I were standing. Afraid to pop the question, the two of us looked in his direction and, in unison, we timidly quieried. "Well?" Glenn proudly held up two fingers. Jeff and I were delighted. "Let the celebration begin," I said while high-fives floated through the air as if we had just won the Super Bowl.

Back to the beer, Glenn subsequenty filled us in on all the details. Apparently he had just released the second fish before climbing into the canoe. "That darn Doug," Glenn said wryly. "I would have been back hours ago, but when I mentioned that I would catch a steelhead for him just before leaving the hospital last week, he weakly replied by holding up two fingers." This was the first we had heard of his promise to Doug, and it explained Glenn's intense tenacity the last few days of the trip. In many sports, heroics of this nature usually make headlines. But in the quiet stillness of an October evening in British Columbia, Glenn pulled off a feat of Michael Jordan-like proportions. At the final buzzer he fulfilled the symbolic commitment made to his old friend.

As I continued to trudge through the rain, my destination gradually came into full view. This would have been a perfect morning to roll over for a couple extra hours of snooze time, and I probably would have too if it weren't for "that darn Glenn." I at least had to make an effort to catch the steelhead for Tom that Glenn requested on his behalf. At the appropriate dip in the trail, I slid down the wet grass covering the steep bank — mostly on my butt. When both feet were planted in two inches of water where there hadn't been any the day before, I noted that the river was rising faster than I had expected. Through the dun stained water my feet were still slightly visible when I waded knee deep to test for clarity. This wouldn't be any easy task, I thought, as I walked the final distance to the run I had in mind. Once there, I sat in deep contemplation on a rather large rock. The rain continued to come down. In fact, it started to pour.

The #4 traditional Waller Waker secured in the stripper guide was still tied to the nine foot leader and wrapped tightly around the reel. After fishing in the rain during the previous day, I left the fully rigged 9' 3" cane rod with the experimental cedar core butt out to dry in the camper "as is" after thoroughly wiping off hours worth of moisture. A big, colorful streamer would possibly have been the best choice for this morning, but my fingers were already too numb to make the adjustment. It just felt good to sit in a huddled lump retaining as much body heat as possible that had built up during the half hour trek. Changing flies was the last thing on my mind.

The strategy for the morning was rather simple: get off my ass and start fishing. Anything beyond that would have required much more energy than I could possibly muster, given the cumulative wear and tear of the sun-up to sun-down effort for the previous two weeks without a break. Add to that the uncomfortable character of the morning along with a degree of hopelessness imparted by the hand of Mother Nature, and it seemed that this well intentioned gesture had disintegrated into a fool's mission. At that moment, I was in desperate need of any sort of motivational inspiration to at least satisfy myself that I tried to honor my commitment to Tom on Glenn's behalf.

skate more directly over the steelhead's lie while maintaining the same drifting lane for several more feet. My heart pounded, as it usually does, when I know for absolute certainty that the fly is, at one point, within a foot of the mystical object of my quest. Holding my breath for what seemed like minutes, I waited. And waited. And waited. But much to my disappointment, no fish showed. The fly slowly swung the entire length of the drift, as planned, until it inched into the dead water next to shore. While considering a fly change as an option for my next cast, I began to slowly pick my line off the water just as the nose appeared once again. The fish had apparently followed the fly from where it was previously positioned and this time, with no hesitation at all, the bright female inhaled the waker that had come to a dead stop in a shallow pocket of water without a current. Immediately, like a turbo-charged rocket, the steelhead was out of there.

As the fish jumped once, twice, three times, then four and five — I couldn't help but notice the eagle sitting in the same frame, watching the events unfold as if somehow this whole scene was ordained in a spiritual kind of way. It was about the time the fish came to rest in the heavy current over eighty feet into the unsightly orange backing attached to my well-used, but sentimental Gunnison, that I noticed an odd bend in the bamboo where there shouldn't be any bend at all. The glue seam on my experimental cedar core butt section had split just below the stripper guide. Back to the drawing board I guess, but that was the last thing on my mind. This was Tom's fish. And not that landing any fish is really of great importance in the grand scheme of things, but this steelhead represented something I couldn't explain. I wanted to see her up close — to catch, release and remember. The rod creaked and twisted, but it didn't break. Slowly, the beautiful ten-pound fish made her way to my hand. I thought of Tom as the fly fell free.

Then, with no hesitation, she burst back into the freedom of the swollen river. Two casts was all it took.

Retreating to my rock, I basked in the disbelief of the scenario that had just unfolded. The white-headed bird continued to stare at me. It sat there. Still. A muse of the spectral realm. Immediately I thought of Glenn. At the final buzzer! The rod was broken, another cast would have been impossible. Likely the goosebumps were the effect of the numbing dampness that accompanied the driving rainfall, but who knows. The Great Bird delivered. Of that, I was convinced. I felt the presence of Tom, and Doug too. Shutting my eyes, I also saw my dog. It was as if I were sent another message. At that moment I knew her spirit was where it should be among the all the inexplicable forces responsible for the creation of life and the deliverance of death. Closure wrapped in serenity and peace. At the exact moment I stood to leave, the eagle took flight, as well, disappearing into the steady rain that traced diagonal streaks across anything that was still visible.

It was only nine a.m.

Tim Horton's doughnut shop is Canada's answer to McDonald's. From an angler's point of view, the strategic location of these carbohydrate factories could not be more convenient wherever you may be north of the border. These days, Smithers is no exception. Doughtnuts, the magical manna! By the end of my second "dutchie," both hands started to regenerate signs of life. By the time I finished the extra large container of coffee, reality snapped back into a warm and fuzzy focus. One final mission to find a trinket for my wife, and then it would be time to head home.

While searching through a local gift shop, I found some neatly painted stones inspired by the primitive rock art of the local aboriginal culture. Since ancient peoples were closely bound to the ways of the earth, coastal Natives believed that all animals had lessons to teach. To honor this belief, they carried with them the depiction of an animal on stone — a talisman. For them, this object of good fortune possessed healing or meditational powers. Each animal had a unique strength or purpose. So when they held or carried a talisman, or meditated upon its meaning, it was believed that they drew into themselves the special energy of the particular animal painted upon it. On the shop counter there were rocks painted with a bear, a deer, and even a loon. I then picked up the rock with an image of an eagle inked upon its smooth surface.

I have always been drawn to the allure of birds. Even though my departed dog paid little attention to feathered lifeforms, I often reflected upon how much this amiable canine taught me about the surrounding world. Through her I realized there was a level of communication unique to animals from which we all can learn by developing certain skills of awarenesss. Native cultures were well tuned in to this fact, and for them this bond with nature, and its creatures, was key to understanding life's mysteries. After my experience earlier that morning, I was anxious to read about what past peoples believed about the eagle. Although I could sense what the words were going to say, I got those goosebumps just the same. It was simple. Native peoples considered this creature of majesty to be a messenger of peace from the spirit world.

A fetish of profound implications: an eagle painted on a rock. I bought the talisman of peace to use as a reminder of the message delivered to me earlier that morning.

On the drive back to Montana, my spirit soared.

Halcyon Dream

A rather stately looking fellow he was, perplexed it seemed, looking down into the cold waters of the Beaverhead bordered on both sides by a wall of ice. This is not normally a bird that endures the bitter elements a Montana winter can provide, but sometimes a hardy individual of the species attempts to answer that challenge. The annual Christmas bird count sometimes reveals an occasional kingfisher from time to time, particularly in the northwestern regions of the state, but the odd cold-season kingfisher in Southwestern Montana is usually found basking near the waters associated with one of the local warm springs. This particular bird, however, was awkwardly attached to a wire that stretched over the icy river just outside of town. Lost perhaps. A somber soul, forlorn and resigned.

As the of image of that bird remained etched in my senses, it was another portrayal of a kingfisher, this time a female, by the Canadian wildlife artist Robert Bateman over fifteen years ago that piqued an interest in both the kingfisher species and the artistic expression of birds in wildlife art that has grown in my life since that time. Entitled "Kingfisher in Winter," the painting illustrated a mature birch cradling the serene bird, overhanging the dark waters of a winter stream and accented by a shoreline of deep snow. Wildlife art can speak volumes if the artist's brush can capture the essential qualities of its subject in that one still life moment of time. This realistic work provided a brief glimpse into the life of the kingfisher that captivated the essence of her character. Strong, proud and alone, the peaceful figure depicted by Bateman emanated a mystical demure that has also influenced me for years.

There is something special about the kingfisher. It is the favorite bird of many folks. Even those who pay little attention to birds know well of the kingfisher's attractive grace. This bird's charm enchanted the ancient Greeks and Romans as well. In fact, the Latin poet Ovid's romantic account of a Greek love tale best emphasizes the kingfisher's role in legendary mythology. In his rendition of the fable it seemed Ceyx, the King of Thessaly, was married to Alcyone, the daughter of Aeolus, King of the Winds. The two loved each other devotedly and vowed never to part. When it came to pass that Ceyx needed to see the great Oracle across the sea, Alcyone begged him not to go, for she knew only too well of the danger that lurked in the winds on the high seas. So, as she learned of Ceyx's inevitable shipwreck, and that he had drowned with her name on his lips, the distraught Alcyone cast herself upon the sea to forever join her lost love. But before she reached the water, she was transformed into a bird, a mythical kingfisher. The merciful gods also saw to it that Ceyx was changed into a kingfisher as well, so that their happiness would continue together throughout time. Every year hence, the two would build their nest at sea during a windless period provided by Aeolus. The seven days before the shortest day of the year was used for nest building, the seven days after for hatching the eggs. The Latin added the 'h' and the kingfisher in Latin poems was subsequently referred to as a halcyon. The period of calm and peace associated with December became to be known as the "halcyon days" of winter. This tale must have inspired Bateman's winter kingfisher, for it is the alluring spirit of halcyon that he has portrayed so perfectly in his work.

To those of us who fish, the kingfisher represents the ever vigilant mentor, sitting in the distant backdrop of our experiences, likely puzzled by all the fancy paraphernalia it takes for the human to catch one of the beautiful trout species. Modern legend could possibly make a case for the merciful fishing gods changing the likes of Dan Bailey, Lee Wulff, or Dame Juliana Berners into these sentinels of our waters, ever watchful symbols of our contemplative domain. For those of us trying to touch the spirit of all who have gone before us on the hallowed trout waters of the world, we look for those signs that reach across time. Whether it is water, flora or wildlife, it is important to understand our part in this fabric of existence. When I see a kingfisher, I feel the thread of my life being woven into a colorful tapestry that is rich with tradition and accented with the promise of hope.

For the dedicated kingfisher, fishing is certainly more than a day out with the boys "slugging down beers and ripping lips." For it, fishing is life. It is soul wrenching, face to face survival. In the watching, the waiting and the silence, the kingfisher teaches us about fishing. The ancient Greek and Roman perception of the peaceful calm attributed to this bird was likely out of respect for its wise patience and undaunted persistence, the time honored qualities of anyone striving to become a "compleat" angler.

A Wisp in the Wind

Most members of the kingfisher clan are splendidly colored, dapper looking birds decked out in what has traditionally been referred to in Europe as "the King's dress." There are only three species of kingfishers that live in North America, and two of these occur exclusively near the Mexican border. Although the species prominently found near the waters throughout our country is commonly called "kingfisher" by most, it is officially known as the belted kingfisher, *ceryle alcyon*. The genus name is a Greek derivative from *kerylos* meaning halcyon, and the species name honors Alcyone, the daughter of Aeolus. Though it is the small and beautiful Old World common kingfisher found throughout Europe that has inspired so much of the folklore throughout the centuries, ironically, the New World American species bears the names that connect the kingfisher to its mythical past. In the historical present, the belted kingfisher should serve as an ever-present reminder of our legendary predecessors responsible for elevating the artful expression of fishing to an experience of the soul.

When the days become long, the air quiet and still, and the warm summer breathes a halcyon kind of peace, this is typically the time of the belted kingfisher in Montana. For me, it's the lure of trout that beckons regular visits to the state's many streams and rivers. Because the nature of dry fly fishing is the watching, the waiting, and the silent blending into the background of willow and cottonwood, the focused gaze upon the water for any sign of trout usually reveals a choreographed show of activity that can pleasantly distract even the most avid of anglers. In the long shadows cast by the setting sun, mayflies flicker in various stages of life reflecting the glint of the passing sunlight; caddis form thick clouds at the tops of foliage before descending to the water's surface, and many species of birds anxiously take advantage of the diminishing light, feeding in frenzied haste on the millions of insects a late summer evening can produce. Robins and common nighthawks, various flycatchers and western tanagers all get into the act. Along the river a great blue heron can be seen in the distant dimness standing as still as a stick, a mink slinks from one rock to the next, and the resident kingfisher flies by in a fuss, making a croaky kind of rattle as it passes, taking a perch high on the dead limb that hangs over a prime section of fishing water. This solitary bird has an attitude, an air of superiority, and though indignant to share its water with anything or anyone, it still teaches. For it, fishing is demanding work requiring skill and composure, and this bird's concentration cannot afford to be broken. This is a true angler, I thought; Izaak Walton would be proud. Since I could also relate to the need for space free of competition, I apologized for my invasion into its world.

It was difficult to determine whether this particular bird was a male or female because it was sitting so high in poor light. The male belted kingfisher sports a bluish, but ragged double crested head, a bluish back and the same color belt of blue across the white chest. The female is similar, but she is also adorned by a distinctive orange band lower on the white breast extending to her flanks. Other than at courtship, it is unusual to find two kingfishers in the same area, for they are extremely territorial loners, chasing away all competitors — at least of the kingfisher persuasion — to other parts of the river. There's a lot of water, it figures, no need to crowd.

Although the kingfisher eats a wide array of small prey, its main diet is little fish. As one might think from a play on its name, this bird is the "king of fishers." From a well situated overhang to hovering in flight as high as forty feet above the water, when the kingfisher spots a small finned target swimming beneath the water's surface with its extraordinary eyesight, it dives headlong into the water. Sometimes totally submerged, this extrordinary bird often resurfaces with victim gripped in its bill, or, at times, speared. Flying back to a conspicuous perch, the winged angler then beats the fish on a limb, tosses it up in the air before catching and swallowing it head first. The message from the mentor is clear: keep it simple, no need for too many fancy gadgets, flies, or even high priced rods.

This cunning and skill is not without cost or effort. Stalking the Big Hole River last summer for rising fish, my tranquility was disturbed by the sound — *kerplunk* — somewhere behind me. Everyone who spends anytime outdoors knows that a well honed auditory sense can be a very useful tool in the wild. Applied to fishing, the astute angler can actually hear sipping fish, but this was the sound a rock might make when casually tossed into the water from a high bridge. A few minutes later, there it was again. *Kerplunk!* Turning, this time I discovered the source of the commotion. Out of the water struggled what seemed to be a novice kingfisher, flying back, empty billed to a low hanging limb, shaking off and looking defeated. As I continued to observe — *kerplunk* — into the water dived the bird from the branch, again with the same results. To become a good angler takes much practice. For this bird, it was "practice makes perfect" for the purpose of staying alive; no catch-and-release here. It was obvious, however, that dinner was going to be slim pickings that night. I then found myself wanting to give back all that I had learned from its relatives over the years, but deep down I had a hunch this youngster would eventually figure things out.

Over the years, of course, the fishing experience has evolved — observing birds, breathing fresh air, swatting mosquitoes, listening to the wind.... For me, my insignificant smallness in the vastness of it all only makes sense in the meaningful involvment achieved along the rivers of enlightenment. The kingfisher is, indeed, wise, for it too knows about such things; and ancient civilizations understood only too well to look toward "halcyon" for guidance in similar matters of inner peace.

Each winter, when life in Montana yields to the whims of nature, I often think back over the many summers that have passed. At this point watching birds has blossomed into artistic expression, or more appropriately, artistic dabbling. During the days of shortness, placid and serene, my thoughts turn to fly fishing and kingfishers. I write my reflections, build fly rods, paint memories, and long for the ability to capture one of Ovid's "birds of calm" in an ultimately expressive still life. In a watercolor moment, I cast a fly to rising trout while the kingfisher, azure as the stream and sky, also fishes within the creative reaches of my mind — a yet-to-be painted halcyon dream.

Big Pants

Let me tell you about the Niagara River. For one thing, technically it is not a river. It is, by definition, a thoroughfare — a connective waterway linking Lake Erie to Lake Ontario. But to most people, including me, it's a river. Above Niagara Falls the serene stretch serving as the actual border between USA and Ontario, Canada, appears to be more akin to a placid lake than a river. In this section the substantive current is disguised within a broad stroke of serenity. But after the massive flow drops over the world's most famous gigantic waterfall and then meets up with the discharge from two hydropower facilities near Lewiston, New York, the river takes on a more sinister demeanor. There, the water swirls like the cauldrons of Hades. In fact, the vortices, undercurrents, and swells of this tremendous body of roaring liquid bring to mind an image of Satan's toilet — as imposing to the eye as it is downright frightening. It should be of no surprise, then, that this place is located in the close proximity of the historical landmark called Devil's Hole. To a fly angler, this gargantuan torrent presents a huge, if not scary, temptation.

For many months after the onset of autumnal splendor, the *lower* Niagara, as it is commonly called once the great flow descends the falls, gets an enticing run of steelhead. These are the migratory rainbow trout that have grown very big while cruising the water of Lake Ontario. For the average angler, though, there is a problem. Finding a place to fish on the lower Niagara is extremely difficult — and even dangerous — especially for those looking to hook one of these beauties on a fly rod. There are a couple places along the American and Canadian shore that are reasonably accessible, but others aren't recommended for the mere mortal. "Big Pants" run is one of them, and the idea to name this location as such came after several years of consideration.

A day on the Niagara usually starts with a stop at the local Dunkin' Donuts. But ever since the American Medical Association made the ultimate declaration that obesity had become a national epidemic, I can't say that gulping a sugared "old fashioned" was done anymore without guilt. The proclamation was good news for diet programs, but bad news for doughnut shops. Though many of us are affected by this health alert, I constantly find myself asking what's the point of a good fishing trip if you can't stop at a Krispy Kreme or two along the way.

Apparently, though, statistics don't lie, and as I was downing the last bite of a peanut stick one day before heading to the river, I got to thinking about the implication of this edict for today's young folks. Ever since video games and the Internet have replaced sandlot ballgames and a walk to a local river with a fishing rod, they say children today just aren't active as they used to be. This may be true for some kids, but all I know is that the older teen I observed a few weeks earlier in Denver cruising down the edge of twelve cement stairs on his skateboard seemed to be in great shape, and the stunt was definitely breath-taking.

In my day, as the old cliché goes, kids weren't quite so bold. Occasionally, a few of us would ride our bikes down a smooth country road with "no hands" gripping the bar. In wintertime these same foolhardy souls would build a pile of snow at the base of a dinky hill and dare to soar over it on a two-runner sled with the speed of a slow motion replay. But the most brazen my cronies and I would ever get in our lives of reckless abandon was to sneak up behind Peggy McMahon, tug her pigtails, and then run for nearest cover. The fact that she was the daughter of a plumber with hands like vise grips added substantially to the risk. Still, that danger didn't quite compare to the feats of today's kids, which include activities like riding a mountain bike down a sheer rocky incline or catching air while snowboarding a snowy slope at sixty miles per hour.

I have to say, however, the most impressive aspect of these born-again Evel Knievels is not the daring of their everyday stunts. It's not the metal hanging from various holes drilled in their bodies, the colorful riot of hair, or even the tattoos painted on sundry parts of their anatomy. For me, it is the size of their pants. They are very big. You know the type: hanging so low on the hip and ballooning so huge below the knees, one has to wonder why a gust of wind doesn't lift these guys into the sky like a kite. But such are the uniforms of the audacious extreme crowd of the XXX generation — the badge of distinction that sets them apart from those of us who have chosen to live more wimpy existences. The pants command respect. Thus it is with great respect that I marvel at the accomplishments of these youngsters who seem to defy laws of nature and shun the call of doughnuts while pushing the boundaries of what any reasonable person would think is possible. It is also with great tribute that my brother and I have named this section of the Niagara "Big Pants" to honor the "no fear" element of today's youth who snub conventional limitations for the sake of a thrill.

The hazards associated with getting to places like Big Pants are manifold, and they are compounded at certain times of the year when there is rain, or snow, or ice. There are washed out paths, high precipices that drop straight to the river, slippery slopes, mudslides, and rolling rocks. Climbing down to the water often requires the use of a rope tied to a small tree. Along the shoreline, angular rocks covered with a slippery green slime make each and every step a challenge. Great volumes of water push to the bank, and when the visibility is clear enough, the drop into the depths of nothingness is quite apparent about two feet out. Falling into the ravaging maelstrom would be certain death. In the winter, since the water averages only thirty-two degrees, death would just be more instant. But if one is lucky enough to latch onto a steelhead sitting tight to the rocky drop off, not yielding to the siren-like allure of chasing the fish into the nether regions further down river is essential to maintaining good health. Big Pants is extreme fishing at its best.

Since living in Montana prevents me from fishing the Niagara regularly, I do take advantage of the opportunity whenever I get the chance. Last March, for instance, bamboo business took me back to Western New York during a particularly good time for steelhead. It had been a mild winter, and my brother reported that the fish were quite active and unusually frisky for this time of year. Since this is the kind of tip that a serious angler doesn't take lightly, I couldn't wait to get to the lower Niagara.

The north wind chiseled through my high tech garb as I got out of the pick-up that March morning. Filled with the carbs only doughnuts can provide and stoked with several cups of caffein, I observed the roaring river from a high perch. The chill factor off water still in the mid thirty-degree range compounded the initial sting. Given the harsh conditions, it would have made very good sense to consider one of the closer accesses along the river. Trying to out-last the elements for even an hour or two would be difficult. But the decision to fish Big Pants was made while pulling up my waders in full consideration of the body heat that the mere act of getting there would generate. During the process of tying up the laces on my wading shoes, an elderly woman approached the tailgate of my pick-up. Chubby in a cherubic sort of way, she was taking a stroll with her rather silly looking four-legged companion.

Without getting into any of the wearisome details, it seems that I have a propensity for attracting an odd array of individuals willing to bare the essence of their very souls at the mere acknowledgement of hello. I'd like to say it had something to do with obtaining paranormal powers after sticking my finger in a light socket at one point in the past, but there really is no plausible rationale for this magnetism. The diminutive being of rotund features tethered to her squish-faced, pop-eyed dog was definitely no exception. Within seconds of a brief hello she was talking about the Bible, the devil, and something to the effect that everything in the world these days is "going to hell in a hand basket." Trying to be polite, I agreed with what she was saying, although her thick Slavic accent made it difficult to know exactly what I was agreeing to. But that didn't stop her proselytizing about God's plans for those of us who dared to stray off life's straight and narrow path. She was a kindly lady who could have been anyone's grandmother, and I continued to nod along at her barrage of comments. Using sex-education as a demonstration of her allegations that our schools are today's version of the devil's workshop, she ranted about the ultimate conspiracy: "Vy, dey evint teach da boyz how to put condepms on der vieners!" At that point I excused myself, though I was hoping that it didn't seem I was siding with Beelzebub. Although the call of the river overwhelmed any desire to respond to her preaching, it never occurred, either, that this chance encounter could possibly have been an omen of things to come.

About half way back to Big Pants, I realized that the trek was much more treacherous than anticipated. Some of the shady spots on the trail were still frozen, while other locations that caught the sun had become ankle deep ooze. There was a small section of trail that had fallen thirty feet into the raging river below, and another that would have plummeted for sure under one step if a person chose to make that fatal mistake. The river itself was more swollen than usual with brownish run-off from a winter's worth of Western New York snowmelt. The thunderous drone of exploding water convulsing in massive gyrations made my heart pound with the fear that I really shouldn't be doing this — especially alone.

Upon arriving at my destination, I pulled out a rope, strung it to the base of a tree, and then held on to slide my way to the river's edge. I had passed several better places to fish along the trail. So why, I thought, was it so important to get to Big Pants? The conclusion was simple: *Just for the challenge of it.* Not unlike a skateboarder or a bungy jumper, sometimes the appreciation of life is much sweeter when one is pushed to the limit. And since I don't make it a common practice to live on the edge, even at my age I understand the value of the lesson learned as one ventures outside a zone of comfort. Standing next to the river, I shivered. It scared the hell out of me.

Coming to my senses, I examined the situation. In that immense volume of water, there were only a few fishable windows within the swirls to swing one's fly close to shore. Landing a steelhead would be impossible unless the fish could be dragged to a small patch of slack above the drift. Accordingly, I attached an orange globug to twenty-pound test tippet with enough strength, if needed, to muscle the quarry upriver. For some reason, I don't like to fish with two flies. But on this day a white bunny spey was added on an eight-inch dropper tied to the bend of the globug — just for extra measure. The logic behind this move seemed obvious. I figured it would appear that the bait imitation was chasing an egg, thus readily attracting the attention of any unsuspecting steelhead. Although the bunny spey had been tied onto a stout saltwater hook with a pinched barb, I felt the need to sharpen the point before sending it into the depths. Once ready, the eight-weight line was stripped off the reel and with one flip, the rig rolled into the roiling rampage. It took several tries before gaining the right feel. After three casts a steelhead boiled to the surface in one of the huge swells. The wind had shifted; so its chilling fury was blocked a bit, and the sky had become a slate-gray wash during the hike. All things considered, it was turning out to be a perfect steelhead kind of day.

When a fish grabbed my fly after only ten minutes of effort, I was stunned. The relentless roar of the river then took on an ominous sense of urgency. "Do not chase it!" I shouted to remind myself not to make a stupid decision if the fish decided to bolt down river. Fortunately, the steelhead showed no interest in retreating to the indescribable dynamo of unfathomable power below my position. It just sat like a bowling ball in the broken current near the drop off. At that point the only strategy was to deliberately haul the weighty creature up into the slower backwash. The tactic worked; and once there, the fight began. It was a toe to toe, drawn-out slugfest. At one point the fish came into full view, and it was a colorful, big headed, heavy-backed male of at least twelve pounds. The egg pattern was firmly attached to the jaw with the bunny spey dangling behind. The battle was give and take for a while, but ultimately the cold water quelled the enthusiasm of the rather hefty buck. From where I was standing, there was only one location to land the fish upon the slick, angular rip-rap, and it was precarious. When the time came, the only option was to put one foot on the ledge in the river and firmly plant the knee of my other leg upon the shore between the rocks. It was critical to keep my center of balance directed toward land. So as the gorgeous male inched toward my hand, I grabbed the leader and reached for the globug.

At that exact instant the steelhead took off. The leader broke just above the globug. Immediately, something else went terribly wrong. In the same motion the trailing bunny spey buried itself in the middle finger of my left hand. It was only then that I remembered why I don't like using a dropper. My center of balance was also jostled off center, but I quickly readjusted and held on for dear life. Since the leader connecting the fly in the fish's mouth to the fly stuck in the digit on my left hand could not be reached without falling in, the only choice was to fight the twelve-pounder again — this time with my finger. It was a tug-o-war. The devilish fish was pulling me toward the jaws of hell, and I was hanging on by a fingernail. The fly had scraped bone and lodged into the meaty portion of my appendage, but the cold water made my hand numb. I felt nothing. This part of the fight lasted for a few minutes until the mighty rainbow was slowly brought into the range where I was able to secure it and remove the egg pattern from its maw in one death-defying lunge. The fish eagerly swam away.

Examining the damage to my left hand, I discovered that it wasn't too bad. But upon trying to back the fly out of my finger, it appeared there was still a bit of a hump left behind after pinching the barb on the #2 saltwater hook. It would not retreat. So with one thrust I pushed the hook through the fleshy portion of the finger below the first knuckle. It didn't hurt. Not really. Well, maybe just a little. Okay, so I nearly passed out. But I quickly came to my senses — as if my life depended upon it. The hook then needed to be snipped with wire cutters and removed, but my pliers were nowhere to be found. The fish were on the take and I had a giant fly sprouting from my finger like an ornament on a Christmas tree! Undaunted, I walked back to the same spot where the steelhead took, made one cast, and then visualized the possible consequences of my actions if another fish took off down river after some excess fly line wrapped around the protruding bait pattern planted in my finger. It could have been shock, but the very thought made me shiver one more time.

The hike back was as perilous as the effort it took to get to Big Pants in the first place. But fatigue had set in; consequently, the return seemed much longer. Additionally, the fly grabbed every branch along the path as my digit began to swell. But there was something more going on inside my head. I looked out to the river that I have loved all my life and realized how the slow creep of age was starting to take its toll on my body. There was a touch of sadness, too, as I reflected upon the day's incident. No longer the spry and limber angler that I still envision wading the rivers of my mind, I reluctantly considered the implications of what else could have happened on this "audacious" afternoon. That sobering thought guided me back to the parking lot.

Upon my arrival I immediately noticed a few folded papers pinned against the windshield of my pick-up. But first things first. It was straight to the toolbox for the needle-nose pliers. Once the stainless steel shank was clipped, the remaining metal neatly slipped back through the puncture. No different than a body piercing, I surmised.

Grappling with the thought of heading back to the river, I started to read the printed matter left under my wipers. It was a sermon that must have been placed there by the previously mentioned lady who apparently took it upon herself to be my guardian angel for the day. *The Devil's Deadline!* was the title of the piece that included all the details of what the devil had in store for those of us who strayed too far from the fold. It even included numerous quotes from the Scriptures to back up the claims. "Woe to the inhabiters of the earth and of sea! For the devil is come down unto you, having great wrath, because he knoweth he hath but a short time." *Revelations 12:12*

With all due respect, I am not a great believer of reading excerpts from the Bible since, among other considerations, they are selectively relevant and blatantly self-serving to those rely upon them. I recently read a passage from *Leviticus 19:27-28* stating something to the effect that trimming your hair or beard or having a tattoo deserves death. Phew! No tattoos for me, but I'd sure be in trouble with the Bible police concerning my beard. There is, in fact, nothing worse than those who back up pompous righteousness with a quote from the Bible. The Good Book even warns its readers against not falling into that trap, but somehow *those* quotes go unnoticed. In this case, however, my newfound friend was a well-intentioned soul, and I appreciated the fact that she had my best eternal interests in mind. After reading a few more warnings about the devil's plan for each and every one of us, I decided not to push my luck. That dance with Lucifer on the bank of the lower Niagara in the shadow of Devil's Hole was as close as I'd like to get for a while. I then hopped into my truck and headed for the nearest doughnut shop. Along the way I wondered if they made big pants for a guy in his late fifties.

In my mind, I had earned a pair.

Reflections

My heart leaps up when I behold
A rainbow in the sky:
So was it when my life began,
So is it now I am a man,
So be it when I grow old
Or let me die!
The Child is Father of the Man:
And I could wish my days to be
Bound each to each by natural piety.

"My Heart Leaps Up"
William Wordsworth

Trout abound in the land where I live, and reaching numerous sections of the Madison, Ruby, Beaverhead, or Big Hole Rivers immediately after dinner for the evening hatch is routine summer ritual. The concept of home water here in Southwestern Montana is difficult to define, if only because there are too many choices. But one of the most intriguing options not mentioned on this impressive list of backyard waters has all but faded from consideration over the past decade. Obscured in the shadow of so many other great Montana trout rivers, this particular branch of the mighty Missouri was once a best-kept secret among local anglers. But these days the Jefferson River no longer enjoys the status of popular prominence as it once did years ago. This previously proud river now symbolizes an alarming trend that is only too prevalent these days, a red flag signaling a growing problem with dire repercussions. The entire West is running out of water, and nowhere is it more apparent than on the Jefferson.

About a mile from my home, the Jefferson River is created by the confluence of the Beaverhead and Big Hole Rivers. The broad flow then takes on a unique identity as it serenely meanders through nearly eighty miles of pleasant Big Sky countryside until joining the Madison and Gallatin Rivers to form the upper Missouri River at Three Forks. It was here, two centuries ago, that Lewis and Clark made the decision to follow the Jefferson on their historic westward journey. Those days the Expedition dragged and poled boats up the waterway. But if they were to repeat the journey in the twenty-first century the explorers could walk great lengths of river during the same period of the year, and barely get their ankles wet.

Although it does not share the same glamour as other regional counterparts, the role that the Jefferson once played in the expansion of our country has bestowed upon the river an endearing distinction appreciated by many who have been smitten by its history and its charm. On better days, the water moves at a lazy pace, quiet and soothing to those wading the edges, or riding the current, with a fly rod in hand while searching for finned treasures beneath a mellifluous surface. The fur and feathered wildlife in and near the water highlight the adjacent willows, cottonwoods, and meadowlands in an array of natural splendor. *This* is the Jefferson that has captivated the hearts of its followers.

In Lewis and Clark's day arctic grayling, westslope cutthroat, and mountain whitefish were plentiful. But along with this human expansion came the introduction of rainbow and brown trout. Although these "exotic" species would eventually replace native fishes (except the whitefish), the struggle of these pioneer trout to survive in modern times epitomizes the changes that presently haunt the Jefferson. For along with these alien salmonids came a great demand for water to fuel the lifestyle of a developing West. Tradition has established that the right to use most of the water in Montana belongs to the agricultural landowners in the state. So by the time the Jefferson's main contributor, the free flowing Big Hole, reaches the confluence in late summer, it is usually the skeletal remains of a vast and wondrous watershed. Despite reservoirs on the Beaverhead and its main tributary the Ruby River, once the contents of these waterways are squeezed into diversion ditches to meet demands that, at times, seem insatiable, there is usually not enough left for the Jefferson — particularly during drought years. What is normally a proud river of peaceful disposition then slips into a sad state of emaciation — a skin and bones flow barely able to sustain life so dependent upon the water that should be pumping through its veins.

A few nights ago I was standing in the Jefferson River and wondering to myself where all the fish have gone. I remember brown trout, full bodied with a spirit to match, once pulsing energy through my rod with exhilaration enough to make one's heart explode. But that doesn't happen much anymore. In fact, the river really hasn't been the same since long sections dried up during the extreme drought of 1988. Although there were a few years in the mid nineties when it appeared that the Jeff had started to recover, the latest dry cycle has significantly depleted the system's brown trout population to paltry levels.

On this very same stretch in 1984 an old timer spent the afternoon telling me about the big browns he once caught on a regular basis out of the Jeff. With a great deal of indignation he lifted his hat, scratched a thin spot, and finally concluded, "Yep, it just ain't the fishing it once were." He carried on, blaming every government agency possible for the demise. Personally, I thought the fishing at the time was just fine, and then started wondering why some elderly anglers become such grumpy old farts. That was twenty-two years ago. There were six-hundred brown trout per mile then; now there are fewer than two hundred.

I suppose if I were talking to a guy from Wichita today, he would probably think the fishing on the Jefferson was just fine — if only because it beats trout fishing in Kansas. But casting my line into the reflections of what the river once was, I can't help feel that the Jeff is hopelessly drifting away into the oblivion of nevermore and used-to-be.

It is true that the Jefferson has been the victim of circumstance. Six years of unprecedented drought takes its toll. True, too, that there are many good people — irrigators, Trout Unlimited, private as well as public interests — working on the Jefferson River Watershed Council trying to seek solutions to the most complex of problems. Millions of dollars have been spent, but the fact still remains that the fish populations have been on the steady decline for years. Other than healthy pockets of rainbow trout here and there associated with the rehabilitation of a few key spawning habitats, the brown trout decline is now widely accepted based upon data collected by Montana Fish, Wildlife, and Parks. Among many other problems, the most cynical of us point to the fact that there is still a twelve-month open season for a limit of three brown trout per day. Fortunately, a catch-and-release on all rainbow trout is still in place, but not without resistance. With the amount of funding that has been spent on the Jeff so far, it just takes a simple math to calculate that nowadays every brown trout sizzling in a frying pan is worth about a hundred dollars each.

I can't imagine what Lewis and Clark would think if they could see what has become of the West since they trekked up the Jefferson and eventually down the Columbia River into the Pacific. Since then, one by one rivers have begun the slow slide to deterioration because of dams, over harvest, habitat destruction, and various other insidious forces. The same script was followed that was already in place east of the Mississippi. Grayling disappeared in Michigan and Atlantic salmon from the Northeast; lakes in the Midwest were netted to depletion, and the massive Great Lakes system all but died.

Over and over, similar abuses were perpetuated by the same mindset that acknowledges no value whatsoever for clean water and healthy fish populations. And throughout all of this, I have to wonder whether there was some old man standing on the shore of all these places raising a voice of concern like that inveterate angler I dismissed on the Jefferson twenty-some years ago. It is just as easy to let the words drift into the wind. It is just as easy to call a man an old fart as to listen to his plaintive cries.

I should know better. Growing up on the Niagara River when it was a biological disaster in the fifties forever tempered my distrust in the ability of decision-makers to choose a path for the greater good. Even as a young child, the travesty did not escape my notice. When I reached the age of understanding, I vowed that this type of abuse would never happen again — especially under my watch.

So I can barely describe the pain, fifty years later, when I stand in a river of crisis just a few miles from my Montana home. But the words of despair I utter drift into the wind like so much smoke from the campfire of a long ago memory.

Ranchers are trapped in a difficult situation. They have businesses to run, but many also take great pride in being responsible stewards of the land. Drought is one thing, but there are other forces at work as well. For years inept leadership has failed to consider Montana's *Last Best Place* status as one of its greatest assets. Folks from all around the world come to see the sights and cast a fly into blue ribbon trout water. Summer homes and vacation properties predicated on a quality environment have become an economic force in Montana. In fact, tourism and related activities is the number two industry in the state. It would thus seem inconceivable that state leaders could encourage extensive development, reap economic as well as tax benefits, and then stand idly by while the rivers that lured the development in the first place dry up. One would think that visionary management should be seeking harmonious solutions to mitigate the effects of these extreme situations.

But in the bigger picture Montana is financially destitute, our legislators say. If they could, our lawmakers would stay anchored in the past rather than look into the future. Indeed, most of them would sell out to the extractive industries in a heartbeat. This fact is demonstrated by the push during the nineties to legislatively weaken many of Montana's environmental standards to make life easier for big business. Coalbed methane operations are now gearing up on the Rocky Mountain Front without any environmental studies to determine the impact of such activities. Also, cyanide heap leach supporters have been trying to get a foothold back in the state despite a track record that sticks the American taxpayer for cleanups too costly to offset short term gains at the expense of long term negative effects. Additionally, unplanned tract development in densely populated areas is soaking up the aquifer with wells that ultimately leach water from the surface flow of local rivers; yet the warning signs are ignored.

Still, a friend from Helena writes to tell me that a fellow employee living within sixty miles of ten Superfund sites grouses about "how the environmentalists are ruining the state!" In a recent letter to the editor another resident wondered why any of us should be troubled by "the release of small quantities of cyanide into rivers in remote parts of the state" since Montana needs the good paying jobs that mining provides. One percent of all the fresh water on the planet is potable, and still there are some willing to sacrifice that for a quick buck.

Our governor (until 2005) is a throwback to the days of the Flintstones. She is quick to blame the environmental obstructionists for the dire shape of our state's economy. She is also from Butte — the city so ravaged by past mining practices that economic growth will forever be stunted by its haunting legacy. I am from Buffalo, New York — a city so ravaged by the effects of a rust belt mentality that economic growth will forever be stunted by that haunting legacy. There is a pattern here. I wrote to tell her that it's too bad there weren't environmental obstructionists years ago. I know, however, that if it were in her power, she would create more Buttes in a heartbeat. "My faith in God helps me make political decisions for the people of the state," she was quoted in the newspaper. I wrote again to tell her that nobody's God would sanction any environmental decision that would jeopardize the health, welfare, and safety of earth's creatures for any reason whatsoever.

The West is running out of water; yet development, mining, agriculture, tourism, and trout depend upon it. If climatic trends continue, the situation isn't going to change in the near future. The politics in the West, however, must change! The political approach that unilaterally makes decisions on behalf of corporate entities has to give way to a more comprehensive water usage plan that factors in the entire community and not just special interests. The do-now-pay-for-the-consequences-later attitude prevalent in Western politics since the inception of statehood needs to evolve in a manner that integrates all competing interests in a cooperative effort which seeks balance and common sense when it comes to water. If this does not happen, trout face a bleak future.

Thus the Jefferson River should concern anglers everywhere because it signifies the slow deterioration of yet another wild trout fishery in an age where lower standards defining our natural world are accepted without question by the general public. Unfortunately, the lower Beaverhead and lower Big Hole Rivers are starting to exhibit the same trend. On the other hand, the Jefferson also represents a defining crossroads of cooperative effort where ranchers, sportsmen, community leaders, business owners, and concerned citizens from around the country are seeking solutions that truly are in the best interests of the river. One way or the other, whatever happens to the Jefferson will be felt throughout Montana for generations to come.

In 2002 an artist friend living on a small ranch along the shore of the Jefferson River prematurely passed away. Dolly and her husband were the driving force behind the project that improved the irrigation system on Hell's Canyon Creek so that fingerling rainbow trout could get back to the river from where they were spawned instead of getting lost in a ditch on the "back forty." Their labors served not only as an example to others along the Jefferson, but also as an inspiration to what can happen when everyone decides to work together for a greater good.

To honor the life she shared through her beautiful paintings of the Jefferson Valley I went to fish the Jefferson on the evening before Dolly's memorial service. I chose to cast a fly where that old timer had complained to me about the state of the fishing over two decades ago. My sense of loss was impacted even more by the river's apparent deadness. The water was dropping and destined for another pathetic flow thanks to yet one more year of drought. Through a cloud of mosquitoes, I stared at the stillness.

But just before total darkness set in, a few fish rose. Casting an elk hair caddis, I then proceeded to land a small rainbow, likely one that had been spawned in Hell's Canyon Creek thanks to Dolly's effort. She loved to paint rainbows — not trout, but the ephemeral bands of color found in the sky after a summer shower. For her, a rainbow was a sign of hope.

After saying goodbye, and thanking her, I then released this rainbow back into the river that I always wished would be my home water. The next evening, after the service to honor her passing, a brief storm produced a vibrant rainbow that hung like a painting over the Tobacco Root Mountains in spectacular tribute to a woman who loved the Jefferson.

In a way I can't help feeling like a door-to-door salesman when he finally realized that his way of life was no longer relevant. I make bamboo rods, spout my concern for the Jefferson, and wonder whether fading away is the ultimate form of change for those of us who dare recognize the truth. Reflections of my youth on the Niagara flow through the man I have become, and that boy once vowed to make a difference. My words now rise above the wind

173

to be heard only by those who stop, listen, and take to heart the spirit of others who once stood upon the shoreline of waters that were dying.

There is little margin for error.

And hope can only go so far.

P.S. Out Fishing

The framed poem at the bamboo shop dangles among the various pieces of memorabilia acquired through years of gathering, a lifetime of mementoes donated from here and there, given in the spirit of harmony and friendship. Our shop isn't too neat, but it is arranged with a sense of purpose. These treasures stand in the corners, decorate the walls, or just lean upon something that is leaning upon something else, each a source of inspiration to all who take the time to look. The forgotten verse that once adorned a general hardware and sporting goods store in Columbus, Nebraska, in the 1920s hangs almost hidden from view under years of accumulated dust. But for anyone interested in taking the time to read it, the modest words reach out with an insightfulness still relevant to the modern day angler.

OUT FISHING

A feller isn't thinking mean,
    Out fishing,
His thoughts are mostly good and clean,
    Out fishing,
He doesn't mock his fellow men,
Or harbor any grudges then;
A feller's at his finest when,
    Out fishing,
The rich are comrades to the poor,
    Out fishing,
All are brothers of a common lure,
    Out fishing,
The urchin with his pin and string,
Can chum with millionaire or king;
Vain pride is a forgotten thing,
    Out fishing,
A feller gets a chance to dream
    Out fishing.
He learns the beauties of the stream
    Out fishing.
And he can wash his soul in air
That isn't foul with selfish care,
And relish plain and simple fare
    Out fishing,
A feller has no time to hate,
    Out fishing,
He isn't eager to be great
    Out fishing,
He isn't thinking thoughts of self,
Or goods stacked high upon his shelf;
But he's always just himself,
    Out fishing.
A feller's glad to be a friend,

Out fishing.
A helping hand he'll always lend,
Out fishing.
The brotherhood of rod and line
An' sky and stream is always fine;
Men come real close to God's design,
Out fishing. - author unknown

(NOTE: The above poem was actually entitled *Out Fishin'* and it was written by Edgar Guest. This is the way, however, that it appears in our shop.)

Such humble truth, I thought, when I first read it. In fact, the verse not only captured the very spirit of those fly anglers whom I have most admired over the years, but with childlike simplicity it also expressed all the hidden reasons I fish for which I had no words. In an effort to share this revelation with those convinced my life had run amok in the trivial pursuit of an idle pastime, I took the poem home to show my wife.

"Kind of sexist, don't you think?" Her first response caught me off guard.

Though I realized it could be interpreted that way, I replied by shaking my head and saying, "It was written way back when." Stammering a bit, I quickly added, "Men were expected to be sexist in those days. They invented the concept!"

Then I got on my pulpit. "I'm sure Mr. Unknown would have been astute enough to be politically sensitive if he wrote his poem in the late 1990s. Heck, maybe Ms. Unknown wrote it. Who knows? The point is that the message holds as much insight for gals as it does for fellers. Make a few generic changes. Just substitute "they're" for "he's" and "theirs" for "his," etc. In other words, bring it up to code and it still rings true, don't *you* think?"

A Wisp in the Wind

Although it wasn't Shelley or Yeats, Debra was willing to admit that it was a quaint piece — if only in a down home sort of way.

So there I was a few weeks later fishing to five consistent bank feeders in the Missouri River on a morning marked by a stiff breeze and very few tricos. The hours beforehand had been a bust. Since a dry cold front had set in the night before, cool Canadian air descended upon the Craig area in the form of uncomfortable gusty winds. Consequently, a thorough search of several stretches revealed absolutely no surface activity anywhere on the rippled water. At least this little oasis tucked against the willows provided ample wind break to make a few close, but erratic casts to several nice browns surface sipping close to the bank in about a foot or less of water. After wading thirty feet out into the knee deep current while working upstream to calculate the proper angle, I then started my tactical assault toward the shallows. Intensely engaged in the ritual of casting, changing flies and casting again, I barely heard the sloshing of an approaching angler as he dragged his drift boat upstream a mere few hundred feet below where I stood.

When he got within ear shot, he made an announcement. "Excuse me, I'm going to have to walk through your water." Before I could answer, he added quickly, "But I'll do so quietly."

"What!" My not too unreasonable response stung the morning chill. "You have got to be kidding!"

"You got a problem with that?" His words skipped back across the water with a tone of rancor. Then, as if cloaked politeness could possibly excuse this intrusion, his tact changed to an unctuous retort, "Hey, I asked you nicely!"

My mind flashed immediately to an incident earlier in the year on the Bitterroot when two passing anglers could not resist bombarding stimulators to the same lone rising cutthroat to which I was casting from a difficult position in the river. In fact, the oarsman had to make a quick maneuver to avoid wiping me out. I didn't say a word. Then there was the young guide who walked his boat full of clients through a stretch of rising fish on the Madison last year barely acknowledging my presence. I didn't say a word then either. And I also didn't say a word when an angler stopped his kick boat at the head of a run on the Big Hole, and then proceeded to start casting downstream to the same pod of risers I was carefully working just thirty feet below him. It took only a few double hauls from his bullet quick rod before the fish disappeared. He then got back into his one man vessel and floated by. "Well, I guess I spooked them," were the only words that seeped through a wry smirk.

Integrity is a difficult concept to define. We talk about it all the time at the bamboo shop. It has something to do with being truthful to oneself and respectful to others — really quite simple. Though a basic Christian precept, there are even some faithful followers in every church who don't quite get it either. But in an era of virtual reality, nothing is what it seems anymore. Lawyers have seen to that. With straight faces tobacco company representatives claim cigarettes aren't harmful to one's health; Rodney King gets pummeled on videotape while his offenders are exonerated, and surreptitiously our perception of truth begins to erode. Then there's Ollie North, O.J Simpson, Bill Clinton, Monica Lewinski, Kenneth Star, the weapons of mass destruction fiasco — from the top on down, we get the sense that integrity is no longer what it used to be. Kids learn to kill on video games. And when they actually do, we are all shocked; yet game makers claim no responsibility. Heck, we can't even elect a president without doubting the truthfulness of the process as interpreted by a politically biased court system. No wonder truth is fuzzy these days, and integrity smells like a pair of old gym socks. It seems that we have entered the age of smoke and mirrors, and what you see isn't what you get. Increasingly, the artificial becomes real, and the manipulated truth we are dealt looks more and more like the world according to the World Wrestling Federation.

In an honest effort to get back to the basics, perhaps I constantly seek a river seam of primordial holy water to cleanse away all the deceptions of a misguided society and the deliterious effects these attitudes have on the human spirit. Somewhere ebbing forth from the soul of Mother Earth there has to be a message of substance appropriate for the times. In the process of searching for trout I hope to grasp the tag end of an unraveling thread that leads back to the core essence of what truth is all about. But in my naivete I have always held that *every* fly fisher operated on this same plane. As essential as the rod, reel, and fly are to the angler, I also believed that integrity was the intangible bond of commonality we all shared while "out fishing." And until recent times, it never even occurred to me that the world I was trying to avoid would eventually worm its way onto the waters of contemplative refuge. Undaunted by my presence, the sloshing proceeded on course with my position. It then became disturbingly apparent that the angler fully intended to continue yanking his boat directly through the shallow flat to which I was casting my fly.

Through his aggressive demeanor I could tell immediately that this was a "feller" who hadn't yet read "Out Fishing" by Mr. Unknown. As a feller who already had, I was torn between the options of mild mannered acceptance or speaking out on behalf of down trodden anglers everywhere who have to put up with ignorant, modern-day macho jerks trying to pass themselves off as

God's gift to the fishing world. In my mind the debate continued as the ominous figure relentlessly closed the remaining space between us.

Since there was no apparent emergency motivating the boatman's activity, I declared to myself that enough was enough. The free-for-all prevalent on many of our Western rivers these days needs a David-type leader to beat the burgeoning Goliath back into submission. In an instant I made up my mind. This time I was most definitely going to say a word. "Yeah! I have a big problem with that!" My reply of conviction rang on behalf of every decent gal and feller who ever sought sanctuary in a quiet corner of mind and water with a fly rod in hand.

I then started my diatribe. "Look, I chose this out of the way spot so I wouldn't be bothered by drift boats. A drift boat is for drifting anyway, not dragging, and especially not through water someone is peacefully fishing. It would seem that the boat should allow you access to much more river than this little stretch I have available to me. Or am I missing something?" I then suggested we consider some alternatives.

"Why are you being such an asshole?" The reply was blunt. He then continued. "I'm going through. Those fish will be back feeding in five minutes. You idiots from the city don't know anything about these Missouri River fish! Go the f— back to where you belong!"

The ensuing verbal exchange would have embarrassed Mr. Unknown, and, I am sorry to say, it certainly did trash the whole spirit of his piece. At the intruder's behest, we could have settled the entire matter with our fists, but I laughed at the inane suggestion.

In the end, I helplessly watched as the indignant boat owner draped a rope over his shoulder and pulled the wooden craft through the rising fish. He cast aspersions all the way up river until he was out of hearing distance. I didn't stay around long enough to see if those browns would have come back to feed; that really wasn't the point. About two holes up river the interloper boarded the boat. He then rowed across, got out and started to fish in an out of the way side channel where likely he would not be bothered by another soul. For his own convenience, he inconvenienced me. A monumental irony lost on the self-absorbed. Since his power of observation must have been skewed by the massive dose of testosterone that apparently had shriveled his brain, he was sure wrong about me. I live in a town of four-hundred people and look like I just came down from the mountains. However, his attitude would have definitely been offensive to any visiting urban dweller. More disturbing, his actions poorly represented most other Montanans who are ethical, good natured "non-city types."

Out of nowhere this unenlightened non-feller appeared, as if sent to test my spiritual aptitude. At first glance, it would seem that I failed miserably to advance to a higher plane; but then, there has to be some virtue in taking a principled stance. We can spare fellow humans a lot of grief by watching out for the rights of the other guy (or gal), a lesson on the river that can equally be applied to the rest of life. If you are doing something that truly upsets someone else, you are probably out of line. I'd say that is a good rule of thumb.

Then there is the notion that somehow the act of fishing is close to Godliness; at least the "Out Fishing" poem suggests this to be true. Although there is no theological proof or Scriptural support, it has been somewhere said that God does not count days "out fishing" as a part of our total time allotted on earth. If this is correct, then the opposite may also apply to those who misbehave while "out fishing." But that discussion is best left to those who are still trying to figure out what happened to all the Catholics who ate meat on Fridays and then died before the rules changed.

It is obvious that the unknown author (Mr.Guest) never had to deal with the "me first" attititude which dominates society today. If so, there undoubtedly would have been another verse or two added to his work to address such issues. I thus took the liberty to write a post script on behalf of Edgar Guest.

P.S. OUT FISHING

A feller ought to see the light,
Out Fishing,
There is no room to start a fight,
Out Fishing.
This silent world has truths to tell,
There are no rainbow trout in hell;
So treat your fellow anglers well,
Out Fishing! - author J.K.

Then again, after reading several other pieces written by the author, I have determined that he was a much gentler soul than I. So I apologize for assuming that Mr. Guest would agree with my assessment or reaction to our modern day problems "out fishing."

On the other hand, my P.S. still stands.

A. Hassall 05.

Gentle Rain

Gentle rain — an elixir for the soul. *Tap. Tap.* The rhythm of nature, soothing and refreshing, evokes a cursory mood of emotion and contemplation. *Tap. Tap. Tap.* This enriching poetry of comfort encompasses our world with an embrace of calm, and for some, a touch of soothing solace. Unfortunately, the opportunity to be uniquely moved by this evanescent presentation often comes and goes without notice. Caught up in an endless litany of daily obligations, busy lifestyles are just too hectic to appreciate the benefits of a simple gift. Trapped in a ritual of the banal, there's precious little time for most folks to take advantage of what rain has to offer. Enjoying a reflective walk, curling up with an interesting book, or even closing one's eyes for a restful nap are out of the question while the *tap, tap, tapping* marks the passing of another minute in a lifetime of fleeting moments.

A Wisp in the Wind

In Montana, we rarely get anything gentle falling from the sky. Blizzards, downpours, and bone-chilling rains, yes — but a cloudy, windless day with peaceful precipitation comes along infrequently enough to realize a good thing when it actually does happen. For me, taking advantage of this rare event has meant keeping priorities in order, while allowing the door of spontaneity to open when the situation warrants immediate response. I could choose to walk, read, or snooze, but on these occasions I get my fly rod and, instead, visit a very enchanting place. Although friends may point out that I don't really need any more excuses for taking a fly rod anywhere, I boldly insist that this is different.

Poindexter Slough is a local spring creek with predictable hatches, challenging trout, and a quality that is very difficult to define. From a fishing standpoint, deceiving one of its inhabitants requires exacting flies and accurate casts. In fact, trying to catch my first fish there on a dry fly many years back brings back a memory of great frustration. Although no spring creek yields its treasures easily, the "Slough" responds kindly to those willing to learn the lessons it teaches. While so many other heavily pressured western spring creeks have fallen into the domain of fly fishing futility, for the skilled angler, it is still possible to catch a trout here without using 8X tippet at the end of a twenty-foot wispy leader. But stalking wary trout is only a small part of the total Poindexter experience. For beyond its fish and beyond the bugs that feed them, the most enchanting aspect of this meandering meadow classic is beyond special.

Many folks, including myself, have fallen under the spell of "the Slough." As an indicator of its powerful attraction, more than one dedicated angler's eternal remains have been scattered here to forever mingle with the complex elements of this stream's alluring personality.

Unquestionably, this is the kind of place that links its followers to a universe beyond fish. For many touched by the calling, every now and then, when all the pieces fall together at a precise instant in time, these faithful are provided with an extraordinary experience. For me, this usually happens in the spring as tranquil clouds build in the early afternoon and the air is laden with enough Pacific moisture to generate steady showers.

After taking a position of observation along a favorite stretch, the show usually starts slowly with dancing drops of silver dappling the darkened glass-smooth surface to the rhythm of my Gortex jacket. As the raindrops increase, the ripples they cause melt into the many concentric rings that are beginning to unfold. Before long, as if touched by the wand of a fairy princess, the whole stream comes to life. In a magical ballet of baetis, birds, fish, and raindrops, the entire scene radiates a symphony of sight and sound. Casts are made, a few trout waltz on a tether of gossamer, and then, as quickly as it began, the curtain falls. When it is over, I stand in awe. There is an unmistakable sense of past, present, and future, life and death, real and fantasy all separated, or possibly connected, by a very fine line of difference. Whatever it is, after being kissed by Nature's splendor, the world looks transformed — if only in my eyes. There is a re-awakening as the dream ends, and shadows gradually take shape in the renewed dimensions of what I commonly accept as reality.

A few weeks ago the conditions were setting up perfectly on a lazy Sunday afternoon in October. Admittedly, fall in the Northern Rockies is even more unpredictable than spring, but I was willing to take the chance. So about the time the clouds were the proper consistency of gray and the mountains seemed to fade into an ashen haze, I was already half way to the Slough with the hope of catching another matinee of the Spring Creek Suite. But upon arriving at the parking area, the situation had deteriorated quickly — as it often does in Big Sky Country. The wind began to howl, the temperature dropped, and one glance at the wild churning of a normally placid stretch of stream dismissed every chance that the status of this current weather system would settle down any time soon. It happens here — a lot! Sometimes I try to defy the elements, but this afternoon I decided to watch from the comfort of my pickup. As it proceeded to turn cold enough to snow, my eye rested upon the familiar wooden sign that hung just a few feet ahead of my front bumper. It is a relatively new addition to Poindexter, adding to the aura in a proper sort of way. The words written there always cause me to pause and deeply reflect upon two events in my past life.

In the early eighties I was parked in that exact spot. It was the first week of July, and I had been casting damsel imitations on Clark Canyon Reservoir since the break of dawn. When the sun got too high for still water fishing, I decided to see if the pale morning duns were emerging at Poindexter. Once there, I began to get my stream gear prepared. Standing near the tailgate of my vintage pickup, I engaged in passing conversation with a group of four anglers. We were chitchatting about hatches and the proper rod choice to get the job done on spring creeks in general when I was overcome by sudden bout of light-headedness. It could have been the heat, or it could have been the day-old doughnut and stale cup of coffee I had for breakfast, but within seconds of this initial wave of wooziness I crashed to the ground in a pathetic heap.

The next thing I remember is still a bit fuzzy, but I believe the four anglers kindly loaded me into my pickup under the shade of my camper shell. They provided water and an apple in an attempt to revive me. One guy wondered aloud if I had a heart attack. Another commented that he had never met anyone who actually fished till he dropped. One thing for sure, they all seemed genuinely relieved as I gradually showed more and more signs of life. They certainly didn't want this episode to be cutting into precious fishing time.

When I finally came to my senses, I assessed the apparent damage. Although my Winston was still in one piece, I couldn't help noticing the rip in my brand new waders. As it turned out, my heart was fine, and everything else seemed to be in working order as well. Once the fellows were satisfied that this quirk was likely due to heat related dehydration, they all headed to the creek. I couldn't blame them. The PMD hatch was going strong.

For another hour I lay in my pickup bed dwelling upon the fragility of life. Seeking alacrity of thought, the words "heart attack" reverberated as an immediate reminder of both mortality... and second chances. It's not that I was uncomfortable with the thought of death, for it is an essential part of the natural process. But I didn't need another reminder either. After enduring a close call in a spectacular truck rollover on a weekend fishing trip a few years beforehand, I figured that I was already living in the realm of borrowed time. My survival on that occasion was merely a matter of a split second, and a lot of luck. As far as the false alarm at hand was concerned, I was acutely aware that it served as another wake up call. Even though there wouldn't be a better place to enter the Great Beyond than on the bank of Poindexter Slough, in the lucidity of the moment I concluded that I wasn't quite ready to cross over to that "Big River in the Sky" just yet.

When my mind returned to the present, the sign in front of me stared back through a dusty windshield streaked with mini rivulets of wetness and steamed over on the inside from my warm breath. Although the board is now weathered and the words disintegrating with each passing day, *In Memory of Lance* is still readable. The memorial was erected a few years earlier. Flowers, trinkets, pictures, and messages from the heart adorned the sign at that time. Although I know nothing more about him than what I reconstructed from the items left behind by his friends and relatives, it seems that Lance was a local teenager who died under tragic circumstances. For me, the sign is yet another reminder of mortality and second chances. With our respective fates separated, or I suppose you could say connected, by a split second of decision, I couldn't deny feeling a closeness to him. Picturing him doing things that boys normally do when they get near water, I often wonder if our paths had crossed over the years.

Through a series of odd choices and inopportune circumstances, there never seemed to be the right time in my life to have a child of my own. To tell the truth, I was never driven either by the urge to leave a genetic replica of myself as a branch of a family tree planted in the vast forest of aimless humanity. And though my wife and I have done a lot for kids over the years, we also believed that not having any children would be our contribution to an over populated planet. On the other hand, I can't imagine the pain of anyone losing a child. It's a community thing, I suppose. Maybe that's why I felt an uncommon bond to Lance. As close as I could figure, he was probably born about the same period of time that I passed out in the parking lot — a mere six feet from his memorial. A pretty Canada cherry tree has been planted next to the creek in his memory. Its glistening red leaves seem to be a perfect monument, standing alone, near a row of bushy willows.

Some folks are truly fortunate, for they have discovered the one place on earth that channels them to a source of enlightenment. It could be a mountain, an ocean, a meadow, a river, or a stream. Wherever it may be, it is a place where every now and then, everything comes together. Mine, I suppose, is Poindexter. In memory of Lance, I'd like to think I've made the most of my second chance, but the evaluation of a soul dedicated to fishing its way through life may not survive the scrutiny of what many might consider a worthwhile existence. But then I guess *that is* the point. I have always realized life's significance doesn't begin or end at the stream, but I now know with all certainty that, for those connected to water, life continues on there forever. It's a fine line, sometimes separated only by a split second.

Because of its contemplative nature, Glenn once told me that if fly fishing doesn't make one a better person, then what's the point. In his mind the journey of the fly is anything but a frivolous pursuit. He passionately believes that this activity should inspire us to live honorably. Treat mankind with respect. Do something for the environment. Catch a trout and see it in a bigger context. Take a kid fishing. Discover what is important. In the end, realize that nothing is trivial, even when the path leads nowhere.

I am always fishing somewhere, even if it is only in my mind.

But more than ever, as I grow older, I find myself patiently waiting.

T*ap. Tap. Tap.*

Waiting...

For the next gentle rain.

A Montana Mouse Tale

"Alas," said the mouse, "the world is growing smaller every day. At the beginning it was so big that I was afraid, I kept running and running, and I was glad when at last I saw the walls far away to the right and left, but these long walls have narrowed so quickly that I am in the last chamber already, and there in the corner stands the trap I must run into."

"You only need to change your direction," said the cat, and ate it up.

"A Little Fable"
Franz Kafka

A Wisp in the Wind

Several years ago I wrote an article for *Montana Outdoors* about the northern shrike, a unique songbird that dwells in the boreal regions of our continent. The piece ended on the notion that this is one tough bird. Just a simple observation of its lifestyle tells the story. When the northern shrike flies south for the winter, it doesn't go to places like Arizona or Mexico. Instead, it ends up in North Dakota, Minnesota, or Montana. Moreover, it is not uncommon, especially where I live, to observe this hearty migrant sitting on a wire above an open field in some of the most horrific weather imaginable. When the temperature is below zero, the wind howling and the snow blowing sideways, this bird remains undaunted. Appearing like a white and gray specter with black wings and tail, its stoic pose strikes an image of unmitigated endurance. Beyond this lasting impression, however, there is a darker side of the shrike's character — a dimension symbolized by the ominous black mask that extends beyond its piercing dark eyes.

Although the northern shrike sings a beautiful song accompanied by a series of trills and calls, it is mostly known for taking small birds and rodents and impaling them upon a sharp stick, thorn, or a barb on fence wire. Leaving the unsuspecting prey to hang for later consumption, its nickname aptly reflects the true nature of the shrike. The deceptively beautiful "butcher bird" uses these ruthless means to survive a harsh climate. Even though I am unable to relate to these tactics on a personal level, again I'd have to say that this is one tough bird. Because of my easy-going nature, I often think that if I were a bird, I'd likely be the one dangling from the shrike's spit like a chunk of meat on a kabob. Nonetheless, this realization does not thwart my admiration for a creature resourceful enough to outlast a Montana winter.

About the middle of January, I get antsy. Going fishing would be a good remedy for the uneasiness, but the conditions here are normally too frozen to get out with any regularity. Although there is usually a pile of work after months of fishing neglect throughout the fall, winter walls now constrict creativity like the ledges of ice that confine a Montana river to narrow ribbons of open flow. Ice fishing is always an option, but nothing cures the doldrums better than spending a day on a favorite stretch of water with fly rod in hand.

Distorted thoughts as well as unexplained mood swings are blamed on the effects that the lack of sunlight has on one's entire being. The mind plays tricks with one's heart and head too. As the bleak din of winter wears thin on the soul and the associated glumness smothers all good sense, a walk or a drive into the wide open spaces is an activity that can usually free the demons — at least for a while. Oddly, it is a time like this when a northern shrike sighting can be very uplifting.

But sometimes I can only ponder the shrike's more sinister side. One day at the bamboo shop, we all concluded that the presence of this winter visitor seems to represent an omen, warning us to beware of the "butcher bird" in real life. You know the type — the person who will stop at nothing to get his or her way. Like many folks, I constantly wrestle this aspect of the job, not unlike the anvil of anguish that seems to hang over the head of the hard-working Everyman on a daily basis. But at this time of year, even the most insignificant troubles take a Prometheus-style effort to overcome. Although a change in direction may be the ultimate solution, a call to my brother's fly shop in Buffalo, New York, made more sense on that cold January morning. The bonefishing trip to the Bahamas we were planning for late March was a beacon of hope that shined across the sea of discontent like a beam from a lighthouse high above a rocky shoreline.

My brother's business partner, Rob McCormick, was all too willing to fill me in on the details. Turquoise flats as far as the eye can see! Sizable bonefish that were just itching to rip out a hundred and fifty feet of backing! Why not dream beautiful — and big? Anything to keep optimism high and spirits soaring through the next two months! As Rob was recalling his Bahamas experience from the previous year, movement beyond the backyard fence interrupted my entranced stare toward the Tobacco Root Mountain Range. Somewhere in the middle of an Andros moment I could barely make out my cat returning from a hard morning's hunt.

Our humble little house sits on the back edge of small town Montana. Out the rear window I can see a meadow, a bottomland pasture full of cows, rolling foothills, and then an uprising of mountains poised as a picturesque backdrop. Like an oil painting that changes with the seasons, this is a view of which I never tire. My cat is gray, and she has no tail. It is a mere fluff of fur similar to that found on the behind of a bunny. She is a rotund critter too, the type that never strays very far from her food dish. In fact, when this feline sits, she bears a startling resemblance to a statue of Buddha — only with pointed ears. So when the alleged movement translated into this blimp of a cat climbing over the fence with a plump mouse extracted from the nearby field dangling from her mouth, I had to chuckle. Since she usually shows no interest at all toward the occasional indoor mouse, which is supposedly the reason we agreed to her room and board in the first place, this display of prowess seemed out of character.

As I filled Rob in on the interesting activity transpiring in my yard, the cat headed toward the open garage door with the mouse still bouncing from her maw. Phone in hand and clad only in slippers, I had to act decisively. Heading out the door to a yard covered with a few inches of crusted snow, I intercepted the cat before she had the chance to take the rodent to the comfort of our garage. In a fit of surprise, my chunky friend dropped the mouse, which, by the way, was still very much alive. Instantly, the mouse continued to head straight for the garage. Recalling my days as a hockey goalie, I thereupon made another move. Blocking its advance with my feet, the diminutive creature recoiled on its haunches. Little teeth nipped at my toes. Eventually, though, I nudged the critter back into the yard, where it finally settled down in the safety of a frozen footprint in the snow. By now the cat had bolted. All this time I was giving Rob a blow-by-blow analysis of the activity in mock Howard Cosell fashion like a vintage clip from Monday Night Football.

My next move was simply to get a pair of gloves and take the prodigious field dweller back to the meadow from whence it came. Just at that moment, however, my wife opened the back door. Although she had no way of knowing what had just taken place, there was only one reason that prompted her move. And that was immediately apparent. Out pops my dog. Well, I guess you can call a Lhasa apso a dog, though I know the Lhasa has expressed some ambiguity about it. Not only does Mandu suffer from a degree of gender confusion, this inherent ball of fur hasn't quite figured out that she isn't a cat either. And this peculiarity is manifested in an embarrassing sort of way. (My wife wanted me to eliminate this part of the story in fear of hurting the dog's feelings, so I'll just forgo the details instead.) At the most inappropriate of times, usually with a visitor in the living room, the dog will engage in some very improper behavior with the cat in full view of everyone. If this is her way of getting attention, it never fails. The most discomfiting aspect of the entire spectacle, though, is that the tail-less cat actually seems to enjoy the proceedings.

The Lhasa is also a frustrated hunter. Picking up the scent of a deer or a rabbit on a walk through the nearby fields, she'll run in a whirlwind of confusion until she can barely tramp home. In fact, the only thing a rabbit has to fear is laughing to death. But this time, as the dog headed for the middle of the yard, I immediately sensed trouble. The hobbled mouse sensed it too and recouped enough energy to make a break across the hard pack. But the latent hunter in the devout house pet kicked in. With years of repression bottled up inside, Mandu seized her chance and made a hastened pounce, snatching the mouse in mid stride. Then in a matter of one shake, the mouse lay stunned. The dog was proud. I was disturbed. By now Rob was wondering what the hell I was smoking. Tossing the mouse over the fence, I detailed the sordid last moments of the massacre and assured him that the story was finally over.

We then got back to the important business of discussing special flies for Bahamas bonefish and the possible need of a new reel. Hardly had we finished the sentence when I saw movement behind the fence again. This time there was a bird snooping around the location of the discarded remains. Apparently the mouse had survived and was attracting attention. In all my years of living in Montana, I had seen only one northern shrike from the window of my house. To my disbelief, number two was getting ready to cart the mouse away. I figured for *that* bird to find *that* mouse *that* quickly was about the same odds as locating the silly looking Waldo character in the middle of San Francisco holding a winning million-dollar lottery ticket. As I related the unlikely post script of my Montana mouse tale to Rob, I realized he was probably thinking that sending me to the Bahamas, a place so closely allied to the Devil's Triangle, may not be such a good idea. The shrike lifted off with the mouse draped from its beak. Low to the ground, it flew as if it knew the exact location of the nearest thorn.

This story would not have had the same impact if I hadn't coincidentally read *A Little Fable* just a few nights before. A master of existential irony and absurd consequences, Kafka never struck me as a guy who laughed very much. But I am certain that even he would have found the events unfolding in my backyard that morning amusing — if not cosmically significant — especially after I had just read his parable. In this case, though, it would seem that the mouse in my yard never had a chance either, despite the fact that it had changed directions. One would hope that the human condition is not quite as bleak as either of these mouse tales would allegorically imply.

"Alas!" I could almost hear Kafka conjecture, if he ever had the opportunity to ponder the Montana version of his fable. "What would you expect?"

Fortunately for those of us mired in the day to day, we are not mice. Although I would *expect* that changing directions might work sometimes, we all know that it is not quite so easy. So, perhaps just going fishing every now and then is exactly what the human spirit needs to contend with the pitfalls of existence. As for me, Andros awaits.

I don't know. Absurdly speaking, maybe it is just that simple.

The Clock

Streets are few in Twin Bridges. A mix of hard pack and gravel, all local roads eventually lead to the two-laner that connects our yawning community to the rest of the world. The blinking light across from the Blue Anchor Bar and Cafe gives the traveler a choice of three directions — all good ones. But for some of us the choice amounts to three too many. Living in a small town can become an addiction, an escape into a fantasy where everything that seems so important to the rest of the world is rather frivolous when judged by our standards. Life in rural America is on the slow track, and we work hard to maintain that pace. There is no need to prove anything to anyone either. Here, climbing the ladder of success has no meaning. There are no top dogs, just neighbors and friends. And, to the best of my knowledge, there is just one secret of survival. When you live in a small town, you have to like yourself — or go nuts as a consequence. Years ago, Glenn, Jeff and I accepted those standards as a key ingredient in what we do.

Liking what you do sure helps too. The three of us live on those roads of rocks and dirt — mud in spring, dust in summer. But that suits us just fine. They provide a short path for a reflective walk to the well worn shop sleeping in a little alley behind the bank, conveniently located in the middle of town. From different directions we regularly converge upon this sanctuary, a temple of devotion, to commit ourselves to an unconventional way of life. Not that building bamboo rods is a holy pursuit, but it does provide many intrinsic rewards that far exceed any monetary remuneration we derive from the effort. Sure, these artistic works link us all to a vanishing past. And the connection to a time honored tradition in the annals of fly fishing history cannot be ignored. In fact, these days the world of bamboo suggests that more and more folks are seeking the deeper values associated with the sport. The renewed interest in cane points to a trend that demands quality — whether it be the equipment or the experience. To us, however, building cane rods represents loftier ideals. The very process symbolizes our defiant last stand, a definitive act of rebellion to slow the hands of time, to derail the wheels of progress. The bamboo rod is our ultimate tribute to lost horizons — the untamed, the unsettled, the last of the best places.

Though successful at shunning the winds of change, we are self made anomalies as a result, outsiders in the trendy modernized version of fly fishing. Since we are caught somewhere in the late sixties, or maybe the early seventies, some see us as throwbacks to an age of contemplation and oblivion, and the background music that fills our days reflects those complex years. We strictly adhere to values that are readily shunned by the corporate trend that favors the rich at the expense of the average person. This is who we are, and it is wired into our hard drive. According to Glenn, it's not the glue. It's not the varnish. Not the skill. Not even the talent. But it is the honesty and integrity built into each rod that is the most enduring virtue of our craftsmanship. As ludicrous as it may seem in this era where all is judged by profit and loss, it is upon these principled qualities that we have chosen to live our lives.

But there is more to the world of bamboo than the maudlin fancies of romantic old fools. It is a magical realm where rods tell stories and time stands still. From a Montegue or South Bend to a Leonard or Payne, whether it be an old production rod or one finely crafted by a master, each rod surviving the decades grows in stature and matures in charm. Once lithe dancers on unspoiled streams, those surviving the decades bring forth a presence of bygone experiences no photograph could ever have captured. The true bamboo aficionado can hardly fondle old cane without drifting into a state of blissful euphoria that provokes thoughts of an uncle, father, grandfather or mentor suspended in a moment of immortal impact. Their eternal casts reach across the years with a gentle delivery that is hard to ignore. From a rod maker's perspective, building instruments with such power is a grave responsibility.

When one considers retirement, it is difficult not to think of cruise ships and mobile homes, golf and fishing. Of course, painting watercolors of John Deere tractors in the wheatfields of Kansas is always an option, especially if one plans to avoid crowds en route to the Pearly Gate. But for those of us who have made a living in the fishing industry, angling has already occupied many days, months, and years of our existence. Thus, perhaps the most appealing aspect of the bamboo craft is that we really don't have to retire. And since we have already done what most people do when they do retire, there is really no sense. Although the bamboo discipline necessitates focused dedication, the skills required are not physically demanding. Like fly tying or even outdoor writing, this ancillary manifestation of fly fishing acumen is an occupation one can continue well into the later years of life. A white-haired craftsman hunched over a strip of cane with a pair of cheaters pinched on the tip of his nose might well be the image that symbolizes the enduring nature of a cane maker. So when the bell finally tolls for Glenn, it is his hope that friends will find him slumped at the workbench. For him, there would be no more fitting end.

Although retirement for me isn't an imminent consideration, I have been thinking about it lately. Not retirememt from work, but retirement from fishing. Though the concept may sound odd, recently a friend shared a rather surprising industry statistic that caused me to stop and think. The facts read that after sixty years of age the hours many veteran anglers spend on the river drop off considerably. The reasons for this are manyfold, according to the statisticians. One may be linked to the risks of fishing alone at that stage in one's life. Despite a healthier class of sexagenarians these days, the consequences of wading in heavy flows, walking on slick rocks, or stumbling in muskrat holes begin to take on new perspectives when wisdom becomes a factor determining life choices. I can understand these concerns. In my early forties, I once passed out in the parking lot of a local spring creek. The flurry of assistance from other anglers was heartwarming. But the full impact of the event did not register until I considered the consequences of such an occurrence if I had been standing in the stream.

Fishing from a boat would certainly be an option to mitigate apparent fears in later years. But, and I know this is going to sound like heresy to my boat loving friends, there is something totally different between casting from a moving object and stalking the shoreline for that one ultimately challenging fish to test one's skills. But it is more. The pulse of water on one's legs, the flush of a sora from the riparian bog, or the unfolding of a hatch as a quiet slick erupts in activity are the subleties lost when one's fanny is planted in a boat.

Then there is the confusing business of shuttles. Launching is tedious and takeouts usually occur at the best time of day for a hatch. Fishing from a boat is an event, but walking along the water's edge seems as natural as taking a breath. Only in the stream can one feel its heartbeat. The stereotypical depiction of an elderly gent with a dangling pipe and a vest full of flies melting into an evening sunset has always been the image that kept my bow plotted on course through life. But now that my bones have begun to creak and my joints feel like depositories for ground glass, I can't say that the idea of retiring to the bamboo bench doesn't have merit.

I have to admit, though, there is another reason behind the weird notion. It is an esoteric concept discussed only by those of us on the fringe of angling lunacy. It has to do with the speed of time as it relates to fishing. There must be a universal law that explains this phenomenon much like the one that deals with gravity. Bear with me on this one. Everyone knows that school or work drags on like a two mile hike through a foot of snow, but time disintegrates in an instant when one is fishing. String together a few days, weeks, and years of fishing and logically life is over in less than a cosmic nano-instant. Since this is cause for concern, slowing things down a bit would seem to make perfect sense. But how? Finding a boring job or going back to school may be an answer, I suppose. For me, though, I know it has something to do with the bamboo way of life, but at this point sorting out the details is still unclear. The complexity of it all hit me a few years ago at the local garbage dump.

Self-reliance and rugged independence is the credo that still guides most Montanans. In small town Montana, that belief can take on many forms. For instance, people still cart their own personal garbage to the refuse disposal site whenever it conveniently fits their lifestyle. Usually, garbage piles up in the garage and around the yard until one's wife gives the standard ultimatum that usually has something to do with one's next fishing trip. Then the drill is simple. Throw it in the back of the pick-up, take it to the designated area obscured far from the residential area, and, finally, unload it into the community dumpster sitting in a depression below a convenient backup bay.

I was doing just that a few days ago. As I stood above the abyss, tossing the weeks of minimized waste that could not be recycled into this vortex of junk and rotting food, I was touched by one of life's subtle reminders. As the task neared completion, I tipped over the last can, and out tumbled a familiar object. Actually, I had forgotten that I tossed it away last fall. Bouncing once, then again, this relic from a bygone day came to rest at the very bottom of the huge canister. There, balanced on someone's sack of discarded trash, looking confused and out of place, sat my battered, well traveled alarm clock. It really didn't work very well anymore, and for Christmas I got its replacement. But there it rested, face up, just looking at me. For some reason, I was struck with remorse.

In a flood of thought I remembered the important events entrusted to its reliability. It regularly came through, heralding a new day. In many instances the old timepiece signaled the start of a prominent fishing engagement here, there, and everywhere. It would wake me early for those long drives to the Missouri. It got me up that morning I flew to Russia. At Rock Creek it alerted a leisurely awakening for the mid-morning hatch, or in British Columbia it would abruptly ring me out of the camper to meet a steelhead at the crack of dawn. Beautiful memories flashed by in an instant; years of experiences condensed into one poignant moment. I just stared, entranced in thought. Teetering on a bag of garbage, this old friend came to its final resting place, cast away forever. Its hands pointed to eleven o'clock. One last alarm. So much time gone, so little left.

It seems that 1997 bucked all trends and every commitment I have ever made to a slow and deliberate approach to existence. I had yet to put it all into perspective. From a fishing standpoint, it was a dream year. Three trips to the Great Lakes squeezed around jaunts to Maine, Quebec, Alaska and finally Kamchatka, not to mention the customary Montana rounds, was all a guy could ever want. But from the standpoint of time, the year vaporized. It was gone in a blurr, one languid river blending into the next, one fish replaced by another. Significance trivialized by repetition. If the rest of life passes this quickly, it will be gone in a blink. The reality struck me! Maybe it was this truth that the aged plastic alarm clock, the time keeper of my spirit, was trying to convey as it lay there in a pile of rubbish.

A few days later, Glenn, Jeff and I had just completed another day of gluing many sections of split bamboo butts and tips for future consideration. What would amount to a year's worth of parts for most hobbyists would be assembled by the three of us in one day. In the winter, this weekly convention is not only essential to our production plans, the stimulating conversation normally woven throughout the effort nourishes our very beings as well. Included that day was a five-stripper, something I've wanted to build for several years. I was excited about the prospects of casting its refinement this coming summer in a serene somewhere. We had just cracked open the five o'clock brew when our conversation turned to fishing.

For many years, Glenn has traveled around the world in search of anything that would take a fly. Fishing has been his life since childhood, but now, with the adoption of four children, he admits that most of his future outings will graciously be done through their eyes. On the other hand, Jeff has taken a much different approach to the sport. Although he regularly casts the rods he makes, his serious commitment to landing only one trout per year should not be interpreted as a lack of interest in fly fishing. Clearly, he doesn't believe in overdoing a good thing. When the "boo boys" descended upon the Bulkley River a few falls back, Jeff set a personal record. He caught two steelhead. That would be a hundred-percent increase over his yearly quota of fish. In light of the accomplishment, he suggested that he would probably leave the fish alone the following year to get his numbers back to average. Of course, we wouldn't hear of it. By beers' end, both Glenn and Jeff concluded that it would likely be up to me to carry the fishing torch into the future on behalf of the bamboo department. Not that I have shirked that duty in the past, but it was now my official task to maintain the proper decorum that the makers of fine bamboo rods should project to the angling public.

With the image of that trusty old alarm clock still etched into my consciousness, it was about then I broke the news. Torn between keeping up with the status quo on one hand, or making the adjustments it would require to get a handle on this issue of rapidly dwindling time, I announced, without any explanation, that I had probably fished too much the previous year. In fact, if truth be known, I had maxxed out. Exceeded my piscatorial limit.

Reached sensory overload. Glenn and Jeff looked stunned, but quickly their shock changed to a nervous chuckle. Apparently thinking that it may have been a bad peanut, or perhaps that the one beer I just consumed had gone straight to my head, they both broke out into a full laugh when I proclaimed that my plans were actually to fish less this coming year.

As I erratically tried to explain the logic behind my thinking, and that it had something to do with slowing the hands of time, I concluded that working more and fishing less seemed the appropriate solution to my dilemma. Glenn then inserted the old adage: *A bad day of fishing beats a good day of work anytime.* In a way that was exactly my point. Although time stands still for no one, it sure goes a lot slower when you are doing anything other than fishing. We had just started to discuss this unexplainable illusion, but a neighbor stopped in for a leisurely visit. We never got back to the topic.

Later, in the silence of my home, I thought it through again. Who am I kidding? Water doesn't flow up hill, apples don't float in mid air, people have to do what they are called to do. Since the world of bamboo teaches focus and control, balance and harmony, the key then is to savor every moment, no matter how quickly they unfold. I was born to fish. Besides, there is really nothing I can do about the sense of time anyway. But as I continue to grow older faster than I'd like, spending more of it building bamboo rods makes good sense. Lingering in the embrace of history while reliving the past through the whisper of one's memories, the answer to my dilema thus may lie in the state of timelessness achieved through a timeless pursuit.

So the next time I am tempted to go to the river, I may just work on a bamboo rod instead.

After all, there is no slower way to go.

Of Grizzlies, Wolves, and Bull Trout

The noose of civilization tightens its stranglehold around the neck of the Northern Rockies. At least that's the way the grizzly bear would judge it these days. It's a numbers game. By the 1970s the population of this mighty predator plummeted to precipitously low levels throughout the lower forty-eight States. Most of what remained dwelled within Glacier and Yellowstone National Parks. Now, thirty years after the great bear was placed on the endangered species list, the grizzly population has recovered in both parks thanks to aggressive management practices. But since there are no fences around Yellowstone or Glacier, the present overflow population now seems destined to clash with human encroachment that has proliferated around the outskirts of both parks during the same three decades. That's how the State of Wyoming sees it. Too many people, too many bears — it's a numbers game that the bear can't win.

A mere two hundred years ago our forefathers sent Meriwether Lewis and William Clark on an historic westward journey to unlock the mysteries of a boundless wilderness. An intended objective of the expedition was to assess the potential for resource development and, at the same time, evaluate the possibility of human expansion. The mythical tales of cowboys and Indians, miners and lumberjacks, settlers and mountain men that captured the imaginations of our youth were the direct result of Lewis and Clark's explorations. Epic accounts of cattle drives, gold rushes, wagon trains, logging camps, and shoot-outs at the "OK Corral" wove a romantic thread back to those times, but the true consequences of this massive attempt to tame the Wild West were never part of those stories.

It didn't happen overnight, but it happened. Indigenous peoples were relegated to reservations; incredible numbers of wildlife were beat into submission or substantially eradicated, and new fences were erected that dissected a large portion of openness into a "mine and yours" way of thinking. By the middle of the twentieth century, the first round of the expansion was complete. Small towns and a few cities dotting a vast area of the West serviced a population that seemed much too small for all that land. In an effort to totally dominate nature, less practical wildlife were driven to the high country wildernesses, and newly created national parks became penultimate zoos for a nation intent on supreme control of its environs. And since there was no need for wolves, they were exterminated.

In 1974 I embarked upon a journey that would change my life. In an existence that, up to that point, had nowhere to go but up, my options were as plentiful as fish in a hatchery. Thinking back upon it, heading to Margaritaville may have been as good a choice as any; but my guitar skills were never that well honed, nor did I get along too much with tequila. On the other hand, hooking up with Lani Waller on a sojourn to all the great steelhead rivers of the world might have been a better bet, though this was an alternative I never considered either. For me, it was another road that beckoned, rather, an obscure fork on a path that could have gone just about anywhere. Although I could blame Joe Brooks for the obsession, the yearning to find a Dolly Varden tugging at the end of a fly line came from within me, and this yen blossomed into a passion of cosmic importance. Ultimately, it was the call of this unlikely fish that guided my improbable quest.

In his book *Trout Fishing* Joe never talked about the Dolly too much, and even then he implied that it was a fish caught incidentally by those throwing streamers (or lures) in water occupied by the exquisite westslope cutthroat. But there was something about the picture in the book. Although the six-pound char was dead, hanging on a branch, and the probable victim of the spin fisherman casting from the nearby shoreline of the Flathead River, the spectacular backdrop of Northwestern Montana piqued my interest. It may have been the fish. It may have been the scenery. Or it could have been the challenge of pursuing a creature that seemed to be an enigma even to the legendary Joe Brooks. Whatever it was, a strange force pulled like a magnet in a direction that eventually led to where I am right at this moment — sitting here, writing a story about it so many years later.

Without getting into many of the details, I started a new life when I set out to find a Dolly of similar proportions to the one in the photo. But the zig and zag of my meandering from Salt Lake to Montana never did lead to the Flathead. As one tip led to another, eventually the highway headed out of Western Montana and into the Idaho Panhandle. It was there that I finally did catch an eighteen-incher out of a tributary flowing into Priest Lake. At the time I didn't realize that *that* piece of water was permanently closed to protect a dwindling population of Dolly Varden, and the implications of this regulation didn't register immediately when I did find out. Aside from the dubious ethics of the person who guided me to illegal water in the first place, there was no comprehension at all about why the Dolly Varden was being safeguarded from folks like me. Consequently, it took several seasons before the big picture became clear.

But one by one the pieces started to fall into place. I found that there once was an abundant population of Dolly Varden throughout this entire region of the Rockies west of the continental divide, but it seems there was an "out-of-sight-out-of mind" environmental policy throughout this part of the country too — and it showed. By the time I arrived on the scene, devastating mining and logging practices along with a network of dams had resulted in extreme habitat destruction. To my disappointment, it was all too apparent that the object of my pursuit was headed toward the same fate as the grizzly bear and the wolf. Looking at the vast beauty and grandeur of this entire region, I remember wondering how so much damage could have been exacted by so few. If this wasn't bad enough, the remnant populations of westslope cutthroat and Dolly Varden that did survive were vulnerable to relentless over-harvest by the same folks who were destroying the habitat. On top of it all, the negative impacts of introduced species like the lake trout, brook trout, and rainbow trout proved to be the final blow for these two native species within a wide portion of their range. I eventually realized that finding a Dolly Varden such as the one in *Trout Fishing* would be as difficult as retrieving an elk hair caddis snapped off on a branch during the evening hatch.

Beyond the many disquieting realities, however, a curious proclamation occurred along the way. Sometime during the eighties, fishery biologists announced that the fish I had been chasing was not the fish I thought it was all along. Though the news was a bit disconcerting, it only took a while before I deemed the reason for this declaration to be rather exciting. According to the scientific data gathered over years of study, fishery experts anatomically determined that the member of the char family native to the intermountain West was a species distinctly different from the Dolly Varden. Once it was official, this latter-day species came to be known as the *bull trout.* Additionally, it was determined that the range of this macho-sounding "new" char extended from Idaho and Montana into portions of Washington and Oregon. British Columbia and even Alberta were home to the newest member of the char family as well.

After the reclassification dust settled, the dainty Dolly Varden moniker would still apply to the char found in streams and rivers along the West Coast. Apart from some subtle skeletal differences, the life history of the bull trout sets this char apart from its coastal relative, since it is integrally linked to the life cycle of westslope cutthroat and mountain whitefish. As for the true Dolly, its existence depends upon the many stages of the Pacific salmon. Eggs, fry, and decaying salmon flesh make up a large portion of its diet. And though a part of me was uncomfortable with this stunning revelation, I immediately realized that my pursuit had taken a unique twist. Good-bye Dolly, hello bull trout!

But finding a "bull trout" of memorable size would still remain a daunting task. Although there was hope that this clarification would lead to better management practices of the species, such improvements would take time. By the end of the seventies and into the eighties, new regulations enacted to protect westslope cutthroat in Idaho were the first step in a process that would benefit bull trout populations as well. During the same period, British Columbia began to manage the two species more aggressively in the southeastern portion of the province, though some believe that continued liberal harvest limits of bull trout have negatively impacted Canadian populations up to this day. It took the official listing of the bull trout on Montana's threatened species list in the late nineties before the Big Sky State developed a comprehensive plan to deal with the situation. Until then, a catch-and-release regulation for bull trout applied to many of Montana's waters; but after the listing, it became illegal to intentionally angle for the fish anywhere in the state. To a guy still looking for that elusive big bull, this was not good news.

In Montana there was always a stronghold of bull trout within Swan Lake and a decent number swimming the wilderness sections of the Flathead River. I never did get around to them. Since the population of large bulls that traditionally ran up the main stem of the Flathead out of Flathead Lake had been decimated, in part, by lake trout encroachment, the chances of a Joe Brooks-style encounter in that stretch of the system had dimmed considerably. Still, over parts of four decades there were ample opportunities to cast a fly for the intermountain char in several rivers throughout Western Montana, Idaho, and British Columbia. I caught them intentionally on bait patterns or incidentally pulling woolly buggers for brown trout. Now and then one would take a swinging green-butt skunk destined for the mouth of a steelhead. And though I broke off a few fish that, afterwards, always made me wonder, none landed would ever rival the one hanging

216

on the branch in Joe's book. Perhaps the most memorable along the way was the twenty-one-incher that gulped a floating salmon fly imitation on Rock Creek, and for years I considered that fish to be small consolation for all my efforts. In the final analysis, an odyssey that began over thirty years ago in search of a Dolly Varden had undoubtedly evolved into a life worth living, but it never led to a bull trout that would symbolize the significance of the journey.

Throughout the years, friends and acquaintances would tell stories of bull trout encounters on many of the rivers that I had fished on a regular basis. Some even landed trophy-sized behemoths. I would eagerly listen to their stories, sometimes with great envy. There were also tales of anglers who registered much disappointment after landing a large bull because it wasn't the huge brown trout they thought they were fighting. There were reports of fourteen-inch cutthroat getting gobbled or monster bulls nearly leaping into a drift boat after chasing a small trout scooped into a net at the last second. Accounts came from the Blackfoot, the Flathead, the Kootenai, the Lochsa, and even the Clark Fork Rivers. More and more articles started to show up in a variety of publications that shared creative tips for catching the elusive bull trout too. So up until the fishing ban in Montana, I always held out hope.

I can't say there hasn't been a twinge of indignation in the pursuit either. I left the Great Lakes basin in the early seventies to get away from the forces that destroyed Lake Erie only to find the same kind of transgressions taking place throughout the West. In *The Book of Yaak*, environmental activist Rick Bass writes passionately about his beloved Yaak River valley. This far-off region of Northwestern Montana is different in many ways. Since it was untouched by the last glacial period, the flora and fauna are unique to the area. Geologically, both the Pacific and the Arctic converge in this obscure land as one of the last vestiges linking the lower western States to the Canadian North Country. Although this distant expanse is far removed from the mainstream of human development, it has been pockmarked from years of clear-cut forests and scarred by a web of intersecting logging roads. Rick's fight has been to keep the last remaining acreage of the Yaak a designated roadless area in order to maintain the integrity of the natural corridor. This is a land of grizzlies, wolves, and bull trout. Their survival depends upon a certain amount of untouched wild rivers and lands. But if his voice of consciousness cannot succeed in setting aside this very last crumb of remoteness so vital to the network of life that depends upon it, then what hope is there for places closer to sprawling humanity. One has to wonder about the bull trout's future as the Northern Rockies continue to develop — especially in light of the damage done in the past when there were a lot fewer people around.

Expanding on Rick's concerns, the preservation of today's fishery resources needs all of our attention, and if we want to safeguard what is left for the next generation, the process will require leaders with vision. It is incumbent upon outdoor advocates to elect officials whose policies promote wild fish and the environment that supports them. Human impact isn't going away, but lessening our impact is certainly worthy of discussion. Every now and then there has to be a line drawn in the sand to save the last essential pieces of a very complex puzzle. It just may be that "wise use" of some land means protecting it for the greater good. To err on the side of conservation just makes good sense! In the end, this may be the bull trout's only hope.

To tell the truth, though, I had lost hope of ever finding the bull trout of my dreams, and somehow this resignation translated into a haunting reality signaled by the plight of the mighty predator within its natal range. Since fishing for them in Montana was no longer an option, my attention turned to British Columbia. Not only could one still fish for bull trout in the province, but stable populations and good angling reports persisted since well before the turn of the new millenium. Although a few trips to the Elk River near Fernie and the St. Mary's River near Cranbrook resulted in a handful of modest bulls, the rumors of big fish, and the possibilities of catching one, rekindled my enthusiasm. That's when I heard about "Mr. Bull Trout."

I have never been one to hire a guide for trout fishing, at least within the range of my familiarity. Of course, going to places like Florida, Alaska, or the Bahamas is a different story. But over the years, I could have saved a lot of "hacking-around" time throughout the West learning much more — much more quickly — if I would have plugged into the network of professionals now and then. I always believed, though, that the point of any quest was to discover whatever needs discovering on one's own terms. So onward I plodded, by the seat of my pants, gaining enlightenment from one river and then another, catching enough fish here and there to be satisfied. But after thirty years on the bull trout trail, something had to give.

So when I heard about this guide who was supposed to be the world's premier bull trout guru, the proverbial light started flashing inside my head. If Mr. Bull Trout couldn't help me, I asked, then who could? So finding the Grand Master of Char became another mission altogether. It took two years to finally track him down, but as one might expect from a guy dubbed "Mr. Bull Trout," he was booked solid well into the next season. It was just a thought anyway; so I let the idea go — that is, until I got a call this past August. A friend who runs a guide service in

British Colombia knew about my passionate obsession and thus wanted to inform me that Ken Colson, a.k.a. Mr. Bull Trout, had a cancellation. He wondered if I wanted to book the date. Although it was short notice, and required an immediate three-hundred and fifty mile drive, I told my friend to count me in.

A few mornings later I was waiting in a British Columbia parking lot when Ken drove up in an old battered jeep. "So you're after bull trout?" He hailed, extending his hand as he crawled out the vehicle door that creaked from many years of dusty use.

"Been after one for thirty years," I answered quite simply, "but I haven't had much luck."

"Man, that's one hell of a long time!" The reply actually had a compassionate ring about it.

We immediately got busy loading his rig, making small talk, and trying not to forget anything in the process. Constructed on a wiry, medium-sized frame, Ken was moving quickly. "It's always good to get to the river before anyone else. Sometimes I do, sometimes I don't, but there's no sense not trying!" His honest eyes reflected a demeanor that radiated intensity, and his long hair made me feel right at home. Only a few sentences into the morning verified that bull trout truly did pump through Ken's veins. He oozed with enthusiasm about this mighty fish.

There was a soft warmth starting to build as the sun poked through the contour of the spectacular mountain peaks that adorn the Elk River valley. The jeep wrangler crossed the Elk and headed up the gravel road toward a backcountry tributary known to attract a good number of bull trout as they headed out of the reservoir called Lake Koocanusa on a spawning mission to the furthermost reaches of the drainage. It was a long drive; so I had time to give Ken a brief summary of my background, including a self-serving testimony to the fact that I wasn't a complete fishing "klutz." Trying not to sound too egotistical, I tried to impress upon him that I actually had caught some nice fish in my career. Also, since I didn't want a maudlin rendition of my bull trout futility as it related to an esoteric odyssey clouding the day, I hesitated including those details in my synopsis. But as the drive got dustier and hotter, I told him anyway. By the end of my story, we had bonded.

"It's rare," Ken stated, "to find another bull trout soul mate. To most people these are just big fish. They don't seem to put it all into the perspective it deserves. For many anglers, these might as well be tuna or carp for all they care. They want big fish — and lots of them. It's painful to my psyche."

"Just to hear that is painful to mine," I replied, "especially considering all my years of trying."

"You have to remember, this little river gets the largest run of big bull trout in the world. Of course, the bull trout's world is a damn small one. They grow big eating kokanee salmon in the reservoir, and many of them spawn in the headwaters. Some of the critters we see are repeat spawners — ten, maybe twenty years old. These facts fuel expectations."

"Is the population healthy?" I asked, noting to myself that Ken never mentioned the name of the river. In fact, he never did all day.

"Artificially so, although the bull trout have always been here as long as the wolves and the bears."

"Griz?" I asked. "And wolves?"

"Yep. Both. And big black bears too." He emphasized big. "But you gotta watch out for the grizzlies. The drainage is still wild, intact, and full of them "

"Artificial?"

"The reservoir, of course, is manmade by damming the Kootenai River, and the kokanee were introduced there by accident. Ironically, there are many more bull trout now than when I started fishing here in the seventies — because of man's doings. The bulls are much bigger too! Additionally, the province had the good sense to put a catch-and-release reg on them years ago. Also, you can only use single, barbless hooks without any external weight."

Holding my breath a bit, I popped the big question. "Any possibilities of getting one today?"

"They get tough at this time of year, so you never know. When they first arrive they are plenty aggressive. That's when some guys really get into them. There's always a chance. I can guarantee one thing though, you are going to see a lot of bull trout." He then added, "No promises, but we should get one."

"One would be good," I replied with a tinge of hope. "I am not big on numbers."

When the jeep finally stopped by the side of the road, we efficiently packed our gear and headed down a long steep trail that led over fallen trees, tangles, and other death defying impediments.

"Get bear! Go bear!" Ken shouted as a precaution. "I love grizzlies," he smiled, "but I don't want to get eaten by one."

After one break to recharge my wobbly knees, it took the better part of an hour before an opening revealed the small river of indescribable beauty. The water seemed invisible as we walked along its edge until coming upon a deep pool of emerald that gathered and then ran along a rock wall on the far side. Primordial old growth filled the steep inclines of a tight valley that accented a piece of water as gorgeous as any I had ever seen. By the time of our arrival, the morning shadows had retreated and the water glistened. The clear sky hovered like a bluebird.

Breaking the silence, Ken announced: "Welcome to my world!"

"Wow!" was all I could muster.

"Look." He calmly pointed to the back end of the long pool. And there, nose to tail, one after another — up, down and across — was the mother lode of all bull trout. Fifty, seventy, probably more, sitting motionless like a bunch of olives in a glass of gin. Enthralled, breathless, and overwhelmed, I figured that I must have died on the way down to the river, for this had to be heaven.

"We'd better get at it before the sun gets too high." Ken urged, and then he gave a series of demonstrations on how to fish the pool with a minimum of disturbance to the inhabitants. Part of the program, too, was to get a feel for my abilities. Fortunately, I passed Ken's test of competency. Then we got down to business.

It only took a few casts before I hooked a fish on a small nymph. It took about the same time before the fish pulled free. Then it took about the same time to realize I had just lost the bull trout of my dreams, but I was too excited to be upset.

"There should be more where that came from," were Ken's consoling words meant to be encouraging as well. But the minutes turned into hours, and the tantalizing bull trout of varying sizes and colors remained in a dour torpor, unwilling to twitch even a fin.

"They get like this," my guide said without a hint of apology. "Let's give it a rest for a while."

We sat on a flat rock, overlooking the river, carrying on a conversation inspired by the mystical qualities of the immediate surroundings. Ken talked about the unique strain of plump cutthroat sprinkled throughout the tributary. Speaking frankly, he continued on about the oneness he senses with the river, and he also shared an innermost reflection regarding the spiritual attachment he felt for bull trout in the same reverence that indigenous peoples once had for the land and the animals that influenced their lives.

"I have much conflict within myself bringing folks to the river." Ken confessed. "On one hand, it's important for people to understand the fragile world of the bull trout. But on the other, some of the people I bring here never will get it."

"All your clients aren't that way, are they?" I asked.

"Don't get me wrong. Only a small percentage falls into that category. But nearly everyone does not understand the uniqueness of the bull trout. My mission is to educate them."

Ken smiled, and then continued. "But there was one guy a few weeks ago. He was from one of those States that speak with a twang. Although he was really too out-of-shape to bring down here, he insisted in no uncertain terms that he didn't come all this way to fish for 'no gawddamn cuttroad.' After a harrowing walk that finally got us to the water, he would whoop and holler when hooking a fish like he was riding a rodeo bull. He was so proud that America was "kicking some serious butt" in the mideast! The flag sewed on the back of his vest struck me in the face all day. You'd think he would have toned it down a bit, being in another country and all. Then, on top of it, I damn near had to call a helicopter to get him out of here. I pushed and pulled. It was dark by the time we got back. What a terrible day!"

I was shaking my head when another angler approached along the streamside trail.

"Hello all," he hailed. We nodded.

"How's the day treating you?" Ken asked.

After telling us about a couple decent westslopes that he landed on his large drake pattern, the angler then pointed to my rod that was leaning on a branch. "I see

you got a Winston there." Instead of a bamboo rod, I was
testing the new boron seven-weight. The guy continued.
"I can't imagine fishing this wonderful country without a
Winston." He showed me the three-weight green rod he
was using for dry fly fishing. We subsequently continued a
casual conversation until Ken tied on my leader a huge
streamer constructed with long white and tan bunny strips.
It could have passed for an eight-inch cutthroat.

"I'd say it's time to give it another go," he suggested.
"Try this beast."

Hesitant to break the solemn mood, I proceeded to
the river anyway. On the first cast with the monster fly, I
felt a surge charge through eleven feet of boron composite
right on into the handle of the rod. With a jolt from
underneath a ledge near the rock wall, the fish grabbed. It
took us all by surprise.

The bull trout seemed very big, and the battle was a
struggle of sheer power. After some major gives, and a few
minor takes, the fish hunkered down and just sat for
awhile. Every now and then it would swim into view, and
then retreat.

"You got a good one there," Ken volunteered, "let him
do his thing." The visitor was enthralled, but the fight
was taking so long that he continued on his way. I was
trying not to think about anything — especially about
what this fish meant.

Taking my time, I savored every second of
entanglement with an entity that linked my past to my
present in a transcendence of wonderment, a liturgy of
pure awe. It took thirty minutes before the brute slowly
swam toward the head of the run, and by the time I caught
up with it, the colossus had inched toward the slack water
in the seam of a very heavy flow. A few moments later, it
edged closer to shore and tipped sideways as Ken slipped
the head into a net that was much too small, while

snatching the monster in the same motion by the wrist of its tail.

"Christ almighty!" Ken screamed in a voice that was noticeably excited. "That, my friend, is one of the biggest bulls I have ever seen. It must be twenty pounds, or better!"

The huge bull trout was impressive. The fore tail was so thick Ken could hardly grip it. The pronounced hump behind its head gave the body a particularly deep appearance. A distinct hooked snout accentuated the gigantic mouth. Its colors were stunning. The back was a greenish brown tone that blended into rose-tinged flanks. There were many small white spots covering the entire body as several decorative red dots adorned the entire side of the fish like a kingly gown of nature's finest fabric. I was speechless.

"Take a picture," implored Ken. But when I got to the camera, the fish wrenched itself from his hands, fell back into the water, and swam back into a dream.

"Man, I am sorry! It was too strong." He was visibly upset. In fact, we were both shaking from the whole experience.

"I am not big on pictures, Ken. That fish was way too magical to ever catch on film anyway."

"Well," he paused, regaining his composure, "I can't think of a person in the whole world that deserved catching that bull trout more than you." As far as I was concerned, one could get no finer compliment.

"If I were ever going to quit fishing, now would be the time." I pondered aloud, half meaning it. "At the very least, there's no sense fishing anymore today."

So we just sat on the rock and absorbed the charisma of an experience that would fade into an eternity of tomorrows. The reverie we shared will forever flow within the waters of a wild river running freely through this untamed and magnificent land of grizzlies, wolves, and bull trout. No one could ever be more grateful for such absolute inspiration.

In the silent hike back to reality, I recognized that what had happened this day was more than just the mere attainment of a shallow goal. If it weren't for the bull trout, I would not be where I am at this very moment. I would never have met my wife. I would never have been building bamboo rods in Montana. Of all this, I am certain. A journey that began with the search of a fish so many years ago had finally ended with a glimpse into the very depth of the universe — or maybe, my soul. Quite possibly, it was this I was looking for all along.

This winter I plan to build Ken a small bamboo rod for his special cutthroat.

To paraphrase his very own words, I can't think of a person in the whole world who deserves one more!

Epitaph

It's gone away in yesterday
Now I find myself on the mountainside
Where the rivers change directions
Across the Great Divide

"Across the Great Divide"
Kate Wolf

On the day before my father's funeral the weather was blustery, a cold gray tempest accentuated by the numbing chill of a harsh wind typical of December in Western New York. But I walked down to the river anyway. Once there, I stood and stared. The water churned, an explosion of froth writhing in blue darkness, as the reckless whitecaps sent me into an uncontrollable shiver. My intention was to visit the old cement dock that was such an important

229

force in my youth. It was just something I needed to do. There are few places on the planet anymore where one can go that are exactly the same as they were fifty years ago. But these days I can still return to the old dock that juts into the Niagara, put my fanny on the very spot that I sat when I was eight years old, and push the re-run button of my life. There is something comforting in that. And to me "the dock" is as much a symbol of all that has changed since that time as it is a powerful reminder of everything that has remained the same.

The conditions were too harsh to stay very long. I first envisioned my grandfather plunking worms for the wide variety of fish that he always seemed to catch when he took me and my cousin Paul there on those warm summer evenings in the fifties. I then touched the place where my grandmother once sat in her lawn chair, close by, so that she could grab one of us if we were ever on the verge of slipping into the watery domain on either side of the cement structure. That morning my mind went back four years to the day when my father expressed a desire to go fishing with me at the dock on one of my regular visits to the area. This is something we never did as adults, but it was obvious my father wanted to connect in a realm that was very important to me. Mom said that he had been talking about doing it for quite awhile. Although it was difficult for him to bend his arthritic knees, get situated, and then sit on the edge of the hard surface, we spent a few hours casting lures, chatting about the days we use to spend on the river, and waiting for fish that never bit.

He was once a big man, as strong in temperament as he was in appearance, but it was only then that I realized how the slow creep of age had transformed him into a being of vulnerability. "Remember the northern pike that ate your perch way back when we were fishing in the boat with uncle Nick," he recollected as our memories both drifted to the first time that I ever went fishing. "Those were the days!" I replied with an old cliche, wishing I could be a kid with him just one more time. Mostly, we just sat there and fished without a word. By the time of my next visit, Dad's health had slipped to the point that we would never be able to fish again.

I stood on the dock that morning in the spray of a chilling mist erupting from the rolling breakers that curled under like gnarled fingers holding on to a piece of the past. Through the dirge of a stinging gale I listened closely for the sound of the train that always captivated my cousin and me when we were kids. Canada lies on the opposite shore of the Niagara, and for half a century I have made a point to look for what I now call that "phantom train" somewhere in the distance. Just beyond view of the far-off shoreline there is a track, and on cloudy, humid days the sound of an enchanting whistle attached to a rumbling diesel would travel through the dense air so loudly that it didn't seem possible not to see it. It was a mystery, but my imagination was always filled with wonder. On moisture-laden nights I could even hear the train clearly from the bedroom of my youth. I figured that it was just a matter of time before it would come into full view. Maybe that's why I loved the rain so much. In *At the River's Edge* I finally concluded that "the phantom" will appear only when it is my time to see it. On this day, however, the wind muted any chance of hearing even the whistle, but I strained to listen anyway.

Upon walking back to the place that I still refer to as "home," I reminisced about the letter sent by a friend from Michigan during the summer past. Bud Kanouse was a retired dentist and a notable wildlife artist from Grand Rapids. I met Bud in Twin Bridges after he built a summer home near Sheridan. He was a great supporter of our local Trout Unlimited Chapter and he loved Winston bamboo rods. The letter was a somber one because Bud was dying of cancer. But despite this tragic circumstance, he still took the time to thank me for the copy of my book. To return the favor, my friend then sent along an unpublished tale that would share with me a part of his past. I read *Sex, Insects, and the Beginning of Another Season* as if I were accompanying him on a final fishing trip to his favorite place in the whole world — the "Holy Water" of the Au Sable. Sadly, the last words Bud would ever say to me were written in his letter: "Thanks for taking me back through my trout life in your stories, particularly when I am beginning to see the phantom train." He died a little over a month before my father passed away.

Walking along the old road where I grew up, I kicked a few stones lying here and there at the edge of the blacktop. For a brief moment I saw both Paul and myself riding our bikes down to the river with our fishing poles straddled on the handlebars. I could even hear my Dad calling. "Jer, let's practice your batting in the yard." Or "Jer, would you cut the lawn please." Or, "Jer, let's fix your reel." His words echoed through the wind as if they will always be hanging in the neighborhood like apples on a tree. But now, it is final. Those days are gone forever, though, I know, the memories will continue to live on until I die. My greatest regret is not building a bamboo rod for the man who made me what I am. Probably he would never have used it, but I know he would have loved the gesture. Then again, if that is the only regret with regard to my father, I suppose that I am very fortunate.

The rain fell hard the night before I would drive back to Montana a few weeks prior to his death. "Want to see the rain, Dad?" I asked. He loved rain as much as I did.

"Yes." He replied in a distant tone. He was very disabled and needed help getting to the front door. I opened it, and together we watched it pour.

"Smell it, Dad?" Referring to the scent of freshness that always accents a new storm.

"Yes, it smells good," he said as if the stimulus triggered a lifetime of memories.

And just at that moment, through the densely charged atmosphere, I heard the phantom train blow its whistle. I believe my father saw it.

A week after I had returned to my Montana home, Dad passed away.

Standing beside his grave on the cold December morning of his memorial service I remembered the words of a song I had recently heard by Dave Matthews.

The tune played over and over in my head. But among so many other peaceful prayers and epitaphs, its words conveyed my deepest wish. After my father was laid to rest, I hoped, as the song expressed, they buried him so that he would always be able to "feel the rain."

The Divining Rod

It has been well over a decade since the movie *A River Runs Through It* debuted in Bozeman that early October evening back in 1992. I remember the day well. But instead of watching the presentation about the Big Blackfoot, I decided to spend the same weekend fishing that legendary river in commemoration of the momentous occasion. In fact, it wasn't until the end of November that I would first view the film, and that was with my parents during Thanksgiving weekend. Since my brother and I have spent a lifetime fishing together, the obvious thread that united our family to the significance of the story was acknowledged only by an unspoken understanding. Like so many others, I was moved. Ultimately, *the movie* became a modern icon that would inspire the quest of those of us searching for that special something found only along a flowing river.

A Wisp in the Wind

At the time, few realized the long-lasting impact that *the movie* would have on fly fishing, though inside sources told me Robert Redford was privately concerned that what did happen would happen. It started innocently enough. In the aftermath, rivers filled with an eclectic gathering of those seeking that certain *esprit de corps* triggered by the tale of Norman Maclean and his family. Over time, however, it became apparent that the ambitions of some were not quite so virtuous when compared to the noble standards of the author. To those looking "under the rocks" for "the words" left behind as well as to those who had already made those abstract words theirs, the resultant web of confusion, commercialism, crowding, and conflict gave rise to much frustration and disenchantment throughout the years.

Early on, complainers kept to themselves. But as time clicked by, it became more obvious that the changes occurring on our rivers weren't necessarily in the best interest of anyone. Some veterans of the fly fishing ilk were convinced that too much was happening too quickly. Many believed that, without the proper guidance, the ensuing free-for-all on many of the country's top trout streams would destroy the very nature of what lured everyone there in the first place. Indeed, to disheartened long-timers it appeared that the reverent pursuit of fly fishing had not only become a trendy pastime of the fashionably chic, but it was also transformed into an arena for desultory experts and a marketplace for a new age breed of hucksters. If Redford's fear was that the essence of *the movie* would be overwhelmed by an element of insensitivity, to a certain degree his prophecy did become reality — at least to those concerned about such matters.

Perhaps, unfairly so, much of the change was attributed to the fly fishing industry. Once blending art and craft with a philosophy compatible with the fur and feather style of angling, some believe that the same pervasive bottom-line frenzy driving our economy in the nineties led to an indifferent disregard for the principles of *the movie* when applied to river business. Critics harped that it is one thing to bring people to the water through a concerted effort to sell more products, but it is another to guide and nurture these individuals to act with courtesy for one another, to respect the resource, and to honor the fly fishing ethic once they are there. In some regard it was suggested that the business of fly fishing fell out of step with the spirit of fly fishing. And though it would seem that the long-term benefit of conscientious leadership could only impact future business affairs positively, the reluctance of the industry to assume this responsibility was widely interpreted as a squandered opportunity to shape the attitudes of a growing number of anglers utilizing a limited resource.

Reflecting upon the film's poetic shadow casting sequence with the warm glow of exquisite lighting, the graceful dance of a mystical bamboo, and the melodic unfurl of line over a river of dreams, it seems unfathomable that such pure imagery could have become so distorted. For me, the rhythm of the beautiful bamboo rod and its significance as a true angling art form reached far beyond the screen like a divining rod fixated to the source of everything that makes sense. As if "called" by a universal force to build bamboo rods ever since, my subsequent hopes were to eventually capture the essence of that very scene with a creation of my own. Now, when a gentle breeze caresses my spirit on one of those perfect bamboo kind of days, it happens. As a beautiful trout rises from the river's innermost retreat and transmits that oneness through my wooden rod to the core of my being, I then realize that this had to be what most people were looking for when touched by *the movie* in the early nineties.

A Wisp in the Wind

After so many years, there are many reasons to be optimistic. I have met more serious anglers — men and women, young and old — who have been touched by *the movie* in all the right sort of ways. Even the Big Blackfoot River has seen many changes — some of a miraculous nature. Conservationists, sportsman, organizations, and landowners have joined forces to enact a user-friendly plan of protection for the river corridor and all forms of life that depend upon its healthy ecosystem. Habitat is being reclaimed; fish populations are increasing. Most importantly, no longer does the proposed mining abomination on the Blackfoot's headwaters pose the same threat that it did in the early nineties. Whether or not these changes can be attributed to *the movie*, I suppose, could be debated; but undoubtedly, much has improved with the river that ran through our lives in 1992.

One July day a few years back I took a newly built rod to test the renovated waters of the Big Blackfoot. The sky was cloudy, the air calm, and there was not a soul in sight. The fish rose so steadily to my gray drake pattern that by noon there was a distinct left-hand bend on the tip section of a recently built four-weight. In the afternoon, however, I crossed the river and the fish rose so steadily that the tip bent back straight again from the pressure exerted from the opposite direction. The magic was there!

My motto has always been: A better world through fly fishing. On many levels, it is a holistic endeavor beneficial to both mind and body. I took to the road in the early seventies like a latter-day Jack Kerouac with a fishing rod in search of the thrill that only new places and new waters could stimulate. Not only was I escaping from the perverse way of thinking that brought us McCarthyism, nuclear bombs, and Viet Nam, but I was also running to a land of infinite possibilities and new beginnings. As a sixties idealist trapped in a body of a doomist, I ended up in the

Northern Rockies. And through this magnificent journey of discovery emerged hope that the excitement of fly fishing and all that it embraces could somehow positively influence the values of the portion of society that shared this same interest. Though discouraging as it may be at times, after a discussion about *the movie* and these very issues at our bamboo shop with the renowned actor William Hurt a few years ago, he astutely encouraged me that such change can only be attained one person at a time.

Maybe naively so, but I believe that the fly rod, bamboo or otherwise, is like the aforementioned divining rod that can transport us to a dimension of meaning which I can only hope is duplicated after death. When the young daughter of a good friend was facing a very serious life-threatening illness a few years back, the only thing that made sense for him was to cast a fly into a Midwest river for smallmouth bass whenever he could steal a minute. He told me it was as if his rod transcended life itself and delivered back to him and his family all the strength and calm they needed to survive the ordeal. His daughter, by the way, is doing very well these days.

And after all the years that have passed since the release of *the movie*, I am hopeful about the future. Yes, fly fishing is about catching fish. But to many, it is about so much more. People, and lots of them, are here to stay. That doesn't mean we can't all embrace the same values and etiquette with regard to the places where we fish. But it is going to take time and a committed effort by those of us who share these same goals to lead the way. There is a special power found in proximity to water that many of us have encountered through fly fishing. It is not only essential to preserve these sanctuaries for our own sake, but this is the legacy I'd like to pass on to the children of tomorrow.

A Wisp in the Wind

There is no doubt that times have changed since September 2001. Now, more than ever, I look for the inspiration to carry on. A kinder, gentler world should have more meaning these days than it has ever had, and the desire to preserve all that is still beautiful on this earth ought to be burning a hole in our souls. A few days before the Christmas that followed the devastation we received a sad, but moving card at the shop from an individual whose place of work, as well as residence, were in close proximity to ground zero on that late summer day of infamy. He detailed his pain and unimaginable grief. During the nights that followed he would take out his Winston bamboo rod, lay it under a light, and then let the memories take him back to all the wonderful rivers and uplifting experiences they together shared in better times. His treasured bamboo was the divining rod of comfort and consolation through which he found the solace to carry on.

This is a powerful message for us all to contemplate.

But so was Norman Maclean's when he wrote: *Eventually, all things merge into one, and a river runs through it.*

These are the words.

And for many of us, they will forever be.